PENGUIN BUSINESS
STARTUP MINDSETS

Earl Valencia is a venture-backed startup founder, investor, and corporate innovation executive who has worked in the Silicon Valley, New York, and Southeast Asia. In 2023, he was appointed by the President of the Philippines as an Executive Member of the National Innovation Council representing the business sector.

He spent his time in Wall Street in the data team of Bridgewater Associates, the world's largest hedge fund, and then was a Managing Director of Digital at Charles Schwab. He also spent several years in enterprise tech working with the Emerging Technology and Innovation teams at Cisco, VMWare, and Dell EMC. He was the VP of Corporate Development and Innovation at Smart-PLDT at twenty-nine, and became one of the youngest executives in the entire Philippines during his time. He also co-founded IdeaSpace, a leading incubator and accelerator based in Manila, and QBO, a public–private innovation centre in the Philippines, both with a combined 100+ incubated companies.

For his contributions to emerging market innovation, he was honoured by the World Economic Forum as a Young Global Leader and awarded by the President of the Philippines as one of the Ten Outstanding Young Men and Women of the country. He was also featured on the Nasdaq Times Square Billboard for being selected in the Nasdaq Center's Milestone Makers programme.

Earl started at the University of the Philippines and completed his degree in Electrical Engineering, summa cum laude, from Boston University. He also has a master's in Systems Engineering from Cornell University, and an MBA from the Stanford Graduate School of Business. He is currently an adjunct faculty for global leadership at the Jack Welch College of Business and Technology at Sacred Heart University in Connecticut and the Asian Institute of Management.

Dan Gonzales is a writer by nature with venture capital and startup experience. Fascinated by how entrepreneurs think and what gets them to perform, Dan developed close ties with the Silicon Valley founders and venture capitalists at VU Venture Partners. He holds a BA in English from University of California, Riverside. Dan hosts the *Startup Mindsets* podcast, a platform that dives deep into how entrepreneurs make decisions and can run successful businesses. He has invested in several early-stage startups including Akash Systems, Contraline, Fan Controlled Sports & Entertainment.

ADVANCE PRAISE FOR *STARTUP MINDSETS*

'Startups have always appealed to my sensibilities as a businessperson, because their capital is never just money, but hunger, grit, and honest-to-goodness hard work. Earl Valencia's commendable ambition is to guide leaders in fostering startup mindsets in their organizations—and I cannot help but applaud his efforts, which will help businesses and emerging economies thrive.'

—Manuel V. Pangilinan, Managing Director and CEO, First Pacific Company, and Chairman, PLDT

'As someone who has seen the startup journey from start to IPO and then a sale, I only learned later the importance of constantly evolving with the help of other entrepreneurs and investors. *Startup Mindsets* is a great starting point for founding companies with anyone considering scaling their impact goals like I did with Care.com and now Ohai.ai.'

—Sheila Marcelo, Founder, Care.com and Ohai.Ai

'*Startup Mindsets* unlocks the secrets of Silicon Valley. Startup success isn't just about brilliant technology and elegant design, it's built on the foundation of the startup mindset—ambitious, relentless, and resilient—the same mindset you need to successfully blitzscale. I hope this book helps many more readers build massively impactful companies.'

—Chris Yeh, General Partner, Blitzscaling Ventures, and author of *Blitzscaling: The Lightning-Fast Path to Building Massively-Valuable Companies*

'Go from "wannapreneur" to entrepreneur by embracing the principles of a startup mindset that this book will teach you about. By the time you reach the last page, you will have acquired the insights needed to stand out in a noisy world, communicate your value to others, and overcome whatever life may throw your way.'

—Simon Alexander Ong, author of *Energize*

'*Startup Mindsets* uncovers what I've observed in Silicon Valley for many decades—that founders who embrace these mindsets unlock amazing innovation while living a meaningful life built on global impact.'

—Jojo Flores, Co-founder,
Plug and Play Tech Center, Silicon Valley

'Building companies is so hard, but we always admire the founders who have the courage to go for it. *Startup Mindsets* lays out a great framework on the most important startup lessons that can be applied to anyone that wants to invoke massive change in the world.'

—Dado Banatao, Founder & Managing Partner,
Tallwood Venture Capital

'With *Startup Mindsets*, founders in emerging markets, in Latin America or Southeast Asia, will understand how Silicon Valley works. It challenges us to find ways to use our talents to build companies that align to our own personal missions and the needs of our communities.'

—Nicolas Shea, Chilean entrepreneur,
founder of Start-Up Chile, eClass,
Cumplo, G100, and ASECH

'In this rapidly changing world fueled by innovation and technology, what distinguishes top talent from others is their entrepreneurial drive to make a meaningful impact. *Startup Mindsets* serves as a catalyst to ignite this entrepreneurial spirit in both employees and aspiring founders—accelerating their achievements through shared, applied insights.'

—Heather Yurko, VP of Digital Talent, Mastercard

'Many people are looking for a unique edge in the workplace and in life. *Startup Mindsets* presents a way for us to gain that edge by thinking like an entrepreneur and unlock opportunities for personal and professional growth.'

—Laura Huang, Distinguished Professor and international best-selling author of
Edge: Turning Adversity into Advantage

'I've been working with and investing in startups for many years and observed that having the right mindset is a key ingredient for success. I know this book will help inspire more people to apply principles of starting up in their daily lives and lead them to a life of rapid growth and impact.'

—Mohan Belani, Co-founder and CEO at e27
and Partner at Orvel Ventures

'As a technology executive, I see that the lessons in the book *Startup Mindsets* doesn't just apply to founders but also to corporate change makers, the ones that want to push the envelope and create revolutionary initiatives, which is needed now more than ever in the age of data and AI.'

—Santosh Metla, VP, Data and AI, FIS

Startup Mindsets

A Blueprint to Thrive in an Innovation-Driven and Globally Connected World

Earl Valencia, Dan Gonzales

BUSINESS
An imprint of Penguin Random House

PENGUIN BUSINESS

Penguin Business is an imprint of the Penguin Random House group of companies whose addresses can be found at global.penguinrandomhouse.com

Published by Penguin Random House SEA Pte Ltd
40 Penjuru Lane, #03-12, Block 2
Singapore 609216

First published in Penguin Business by Penguin Random House SEA 2024

Copyright © Earl Valencia, Dan Gonzales 2024

All rights reserved

10 9 8 7 6 5 4 3 2 1

The views and opinions expressed in this book are the authors' own and the facts are as reported by them which have been verified to the extent possible, and the publishers are not in any way liable for the same.

Please note that no part of this book may be used or reproduced in any manner for the purpose of training artificial intelligence technologies or systems.

ISBN 9789815204872

Typeset in Garamond by MAP Systems, Bengaluru, India

This book is sold subject to the condition that it shall not, by way of trade or otherwise, be lent, resold, hired out, or otherwise circulated without the publisher's prior consent in any form of binding or cover other than that in which it is published and without a similar condition including this condition being imposed on the subsequent purchaser.

www.penguin.sg

*Dedicated to those brave enough to follow their dreams
and for those who live their lives in service of others*

Contents

Preface	xiii
Introduction	xvii

1. Defining a Startup Mindset	1
2. Startup Mindset versus Traditional Business Mindset	11
3. Developing Your Startup Mindset	17
4. Find One Phrase that Encapsulates Your Personal Mission	27
5. Dare to Be Different	33
6. Map Out Your Career Portfolio	41
7. Action Trumps Talk. Don't Be a Wannapreneur.	57
8. The Power of Place	71
9. Let Data and Market Feedback Be Your Guide	77
10. Find Your Superpower and Kryptonite	83
11. Real People, Real Relationships: How to Genuinely Build Your Network	93
12. Communication: Sharing Your Story	105
13. Constant Reflection: What Matters to You and Why?	113
14. Overcoming Obstacles	123
15. It's a Marathon, Not a Sprint: Sustaining the Journey	137

Epilogue: Final Thoughts	143
Acknowledgements	149

Preface

'Open your mouth only if what you are going to say is more beautiful than the silence.'

—Spanish Proverb

The road in front was pitch black. It was the first time Dan could see nothing but the asphalt with yellow dashes illuminated by the headlights. He glanced to the left of the driver's side window and saw no objects in the distance other than what he assumed was desert for miles. The car stereo played a Notorious B.I.G. song as he cautiously steered his friend's Toyota Prius at 75 miles per hour down the road. Their road trip fun had paused as all his attention was focused on making sure they stayed in their lane and the car drove smoothly. He glanced at the rear-view mirror and saw no cars behind them. He did this every once in a while, just to make sure. The tank was three-fourths full and there were another 150 miles to go before he'd even consider stopping for gas.

It was at that moment, Dan started pondering his life, his existence. At least 200 miles away from civilization, nothing to be seen or heard other than the car speakers playing some random song. His eyes and arms grew weary as the car continued at 75 miles per hour. Maybe they should just pull over and sleep on the side of the road until the sun rises. There were two options: keep driving or stop and rest. But to his surprise, his buddy took over and continued the journey as he moved to the passenger seat, exhausted.

He felt alive. Despite being tired and half-asleep, his mind kept racing, he had a strange feeling that this place might hold answers to important questions in his life at that moment.

Two hours later, they stopped for gas in Needles, California. It was now 5 a.m. and there was no sign of dawn or civilization for at least another two to three hours. Despite wearing four layers of clothes, he felt the cold and barrenness of the desert. They were greeted by a loud 'whoosh!' as a big rig drove by while they were gassing up their car. It was the first sound he had heard from the outside in hours and his body tensed up, startled by the sheer sound the truck made. Every noise or movement was amplified and he was paying attention to everything. For the first time in twenty-four years, he felt like he was in the middle of nowhere. Growing on the West Coast, not having many family vacations outside of the Philippines and Canada, made venturing to the desert an eye-opener. In his mind, all that mattered was he was safe and able to return to society eventually.

The Grand Canyon was still about four to five hours away according to Apple Maps. It can easily be described a hundred times over but nothing compares to the feeling he had when they finally reached South Bend. It was freezing cold, about 35 degrees Fahrenheit, and he had four layers and a grey Carhartt beanie on. Running on no sleep and an exhausting twelve-hour drive from San Francisco, he was excited to see what this whole journey was about. Other than a quick getaway from city life, the Grand Canyon to him was one of Earth's natural wonders that had to be seen. How had a massive canyon been created in the first place, and what made the view so beautiful and awe-inspiring? These were some of the things he had been wondering about for years. Photographs cannot do justice to it. There's something about nature that just heals us.

The Grand Canyon was formed over six million years ago, but some rocks are estimated to be a billion years old. As humans, we aspire to live for over a hundred years. A sobering realization is that the Canyon will still be here even after we are gone. The bigger question for us in the midst of our humanity is: how will we spend those hundred years given to us and potentially use what time we have to make a dent in the universe? Our lives can be a speck of dust in the timeline of the universe, but all of us can make sure that our impact can create a ripple effect reaching far beyond our time.

* * *

Before, when humans lived with gadgets at their disposal, they relied on trust and communication to meet up, now there may be less opportunities to depend on other people in an intimate setting.

The present is definitely different from what it used to be. Early morning walks to the coffee shop and rides on the subway system are out. Morning commutes to the kitchen table and bedroom desk are in. Startups are working to ensure they have enough runway for eighteen to twenty-four months. Moreover, the employees within these organizations are spending at least four hours a day on Zoom working to adapt to a fully remote workplace. Consumer behaviour has become a moving target that requires adaptation and a digital game plan that can cater to customers in quick and efficient modes.

Today's young Americans have seen their parents and loved ones work until retirement, living their lives on a fixed schedule that required morning and evening commutes to and from offices or worksites. But when Covid-19 happened, many jobs within the workforce became remote overnight. More and more people have realized that they can make a living from home, something startups had adopted years before.

Why is it that we have been designed from an early age to want to be workers when our personal passions mean so much more to us? What if your ideas became tangible products with real-world outcomes that directly correlate to your work? All too often, the average employee—albeit at an investment bank, corporate technology company, or enterprise—feels underappreciated for their efforts and lacks a sense of belonging. Why is that? Ownership and influence over something that you've created yourself is way more fulfilling than the standard American nine to five. With this book, we will explore how creating a startup and being entrepreneurial can benefit everyone's unique skills and talents.

The path of entrepreneurship may be unfamiliar to most because the traditional work that pays per hour and on a bi-weekly basis gets thrown out of the window when one becomes a founder or business owner. The capital source comes from producing cash flow or raising money from an entity outside of the company. According to the Small Business Administration (SBA), despite these challenges of starting a company, over five million new business applications were filed in 2023, showing that the entrepreneurial spirit is alive and well.[1] With layoffs happening left, right, and centre, people have realized that job security is more at risk than they thought, and being the one in charge is the best way to hedge against uncertainty because it places the employee in the owner's seat.

Entrepreneurs are pillars of resilience; they're often down to their last strike, having to build a plane while flying it. Their ultimate stories of growth and triumph are worth noting. Doing something deemed impossible by many and succeeding at scale? Even just the attempt is inspiring. *Startup Mindsets* will inspire and provide frameworks to get started and keep going.

---

[1] Commerce Institute, 'How Many New Businesses Are Started Each Year? New Data Reveals the Answer.' https://www.commerceinstitute.com/new-businesses-started-every-year.

Introduction

'Being fearless isn't being 100 per cent not fearful; it's being terrified but you jump anyway.'

—Taylor Swift

We envisioned this book as we were walking down the streets of San Francisco in 2019. We were coming from a technology event downtown and we both wondered what might be the secret sauce of Silicon Valley. We asked ourselves, 'What do these startup entrepreneurs have that other founders in other geographies don't seem to crack?' We agreed at that time, the secret was more than the investment dollars, or access to talent or technology, or the presence of top academic institutions like Stanford or UC Berkeley. It was something deeper, it was the 'startup mindset'.

As a kid, you get asked often, 'What do you want to be when you grow up?' The question lingers in your mind as you take classes and continue through academia. You respond with what sounds cool at the time, like 'I'll be an astronaut or a basketball player'. These are all noble pursuits that we all dream of not knowing our limitations or interests well enough. Dan's response to get adults off his back was 'I'll be a cop.' Now, as Dan looks back at that response, he realizes he just wanted to be cool and feel like a superhero while fighting bad guys. To him, being able to have fun and truly enjoy the work is what he values greatly in a job.

xviii   Introduction

When you are a child, you aren't afraid of trying new sports or learning new lessons. As children, we have unlimited imagination, a trait that starts to decline when we grow up as we are conditioned to believe things are the way they are and we can't do anything about it. It is inculcated in us from working jobs where things need to be done according to plan. While that promotes productivity and success, it does not always work well with having the freedom to make your own decisions. Regimented processes for getting things done and an endless checklist that accompanies the day-to-day responsibilities of an adult get in the way of dreaming up new ideas and exploring new pursuits. Instead, we highly recommend that everyone lean into the fun and adopt a startup mindset.

Our goal behind writing this book is to demystify and simplify these mindsets that we observed in the innovation-driven ecosystem packed in 5,000 square kilometres, or 1,854 square miles of Silicon Valley, that have impacted the lives of billions of people in the world through their products and services that have scaled beyond these borders. We realized that not everyone can move to this place or get plugged in right away, so our hope is that this book can provide a way or a blueprint for people to finally crack the code and embrace the set of mindsets that can help take a dream and a small team up a path towards building a large-scale business. Most books will teach the readers how to create a startup, but this book aims to dig deeper into why someone decides to start a company or initiative, and the mental models that he or she has to go through to get there.

As someone who was born in California but grew up in the Philippines until he was eighteen, Earl embraced technology his entire life, not knowing that his love for the intersection of business and technology was already in him. When he was eleven, Earl saw the Saturn rocket that helped bring man to space. He knew he wanted to be an engineer. That passion propelled him to go to college for engineering at the University of the Philippines and

Introduction

subsequently continue as a transfer to Boston University where Earl graduated in the top of his class in Electrical Engineering.

Rather than doing a PhD at MIT, Earl started working at Raytheon Company, one of the top organizations with a number of classified R & D projects, which included rockets, satellites, and drones. He was an aerospace engineering geek, but one day, he got a note that Stanford Graduate School of Business was accepting non-traditional applicants from the science and engineering fields to apply to the MBA school without requiring the GMAT but replacing it with the GRE. This proved to be the exception that changed the trajectory of Earl's life. He became one of the first students to be admitted in the highly selective Stanford MBA programme who never took the GMAT.

This exposure to the heart of Silicon Valley via Stanford opened Earl's eyes to the inner world of venture-backed companies. He learned that thinking out of the box paves the way for innovation and that maintaining standard ways of thinking won't yield high returns both personally or financially. For example, he was always taught by his mom, who is a traditional Filipino mother, to play it safe and to avoid failure at all costs especially if it's to save face, which is important in Asian culture. During his Stanford orientation, the head of career services kept harping on about how important it is to take risks, even taking classes that you might not otherwise consider because you aren't sure if you will get an A.

With the foundation of innovation that he gained during his time at Stanford, he embarked on a career focused on ideating and launching new businesses either within large companies or via startup ventures. For example, after business school, he has been constantly building and implementing emerging technologies for more than fifteen years. He worked at Cisco Systems' Emerging Technology Group where he managed one of the first global innovation competitions called the I-Prize with more than hundred countries participating in the competition, and then moved back to Asia where he built one of the first startup accelerators and pre-seed venture funds focused on emerging market needs called IdeaSpace based in the Philippines. It has now grown to be the gold standard for accelerators in the country. He then worked at places to implement innovation like Bridgewater, the mythical hedge fund started by Ray Dalio, where he became the Program Manager of the Data team, and then was Managing Director of Digital at Charles Schwab in San Francisco. Lately, he has transitioned to being a startup founder who has raised over USD 5 million in their seed round and, in 2023, was appointed by the President of the Philippines to represent the business sector at the country's National Innovation Council together with his cabinet.

On the other hand, Dan, having grown up in San Francisco, knew that you could live in the San Francisco Bay Area your entire life, but actually not be 'in the know' and immersed in the culture of startups and technology.

Earl grew up in the Philippines, and before going to MBA school at Stanford, never really knew what this region or culture was about. Even after living all over the United States, in Boston, Tampa, Dallas, and Los Angeles, Earl was clueless. Even if you are deep within the ecosystem where you learn from hundreds of entrepreneurs, investors, and other stakeholders in the community, we hope that this will also be a way for each of you to ask yourselves and see what other lessons you might need to take to further develop your startup mindsets.

As a first generation Filipino American and only child, growing up in San Francisco exposed Dan to open mindedness and creativity. In 2015, witnessing the city becoming the tech capital of the world heightened his curiosity about the driving forces behind what made tech so revolutionary and life-changing. From the hundreds of new companies that were once startups, whose products made their way into our daily lives, he was keen to learn the backstory behind their rapid growth. He'd see people on the streets donning backpacks with logos he'd never heard of before during his summer breaks at home and witnessed a real estate market boom due to the high-earning jobs in tech companies.

He recalls the day in the summer of 2017, he was recruited to be a substitute receptionist at Slack and it was the first time he walked through a startup's door, let alone knowing what a startup was. As soon as he got out of the elevator and turned into the lobby area, he saw a big, colourful sign shaped as a hashtag, it was Slack's logo. The office environment felt techy yet, he had no idea what kind of technology they created or what made it special.

Another distinguishing feature was catered lunch twice a week. All that time, he wondered how does this company have so much money to spend on this? Aren't they brand new?

Tech was the new, cool thing to do, you could tell people were hungry to cash in on an Initial Public Offering (IPO) or do something that no one else was doing. The energy in the streets, neighbourhoods, and downtown San Francisco was noticeably different, uppity, youthful, and techy.

His curiosity coincided with his desire to invest in early-stage startups as he did an apprenticeship in venture capital and started the *Startup Mindsets* podcast. His career has been anything but linear, having worked at Google and as an assistant to a celebrity. Entrepreneurship is something he is continually fascinated by because it is where dreams are set into motion. These dreams then create ripple effects throughout the world.

Throughout this book we assert the importance of how combining a mindset with the operating disciplines championed by startups will lead to unrivalled success in both business and life. We will show how to overcome the challenges of the present while believing in big picture ideas. We hope that you will join our journey to help discover your own list of Startup Mindsets.

1

Defining a Startup Mindset

'Video killed the radio star, pictures came and broke your heart.'
—The Buggles, 1981

In 1981, the world's first music video debuted on MTV. The song 'Video Killed the Radio Star' performed by the Buggles set the stage for the decline of radio and the rise of music television sensations. It is somewhat ironic that the title of the song was literally a slap in the face to the radio industry. Music videos gradually became the norm, which then started to influence fashion, art, and other would-be trends across the world. Prior to the debut, music had been listened to primarily on the radio until MTV ushered in a new era of rock bands, pop songs, and hip-hop that added visuals to each artist. Teens started to dress and style their hair like the artists on TV and a cultural revolution was underway.

Music videos paved the way for gossip and stories to be placed behind the artists and songs on a global scale. The visual element and fact that every teenager was watching the channel changed the music industry forever. The same can be said for when YouTube, Apple Music, and Spotify entered the playing field providing access to music streaming. It's the breakthrough technology of companies that alter an entire industry and people's lives forever. Combining business and technology truly has the power to transform generations of consumer choices. With music's transition to digital arrived the need for artists and record labels to adapt their strategy to streaming instead of optimizing for album sales.

During the early 2000s, new tech like the iPod forced many artists to abandon selling CDs and focus on Apple iTunes sales, which then became about focusing on downloads and streams with Spotify and Apple's subscription service for unlimited music with no ads. The wheel of innovation continues to reinvent itself in modes that are quicker and more convenient. This is a ubiquitous trait of the digital shift, as it affects all businesses, consumers, and redefines a market. Spotify's success was driven by the adoption of mobiles, and the welcoming of their technology by musicians, unlike Pandora and Apple Music, meant they could rapidly monetize through a subscription service for USD 9.99 a month. Of course, many factors fell into place but the ability to provide access to music on a quality product was life-changing. In 2018, only thirty-two million CDs were sold, nearly 100 million less than in 2008.[1]

If video indeed did kill the radio star, today's equivalent would be the internet destroying the TV star. With the band of streaming services and social media platforms—Netflix, Prime, Hulu, YouTube, Instagram, and TikTok—all absorbing the bulk of consumer eyeballs, TV ratings have suffered tremendously. In fact, TV viewership is down 9 percent.[2] With a rapidly changing consumer market, corporations in advertisement and media are allocating energy towards mobile engagement because the value of an ad seen on Instagram is more direct and subtle than the commercials on TV. What has corporations scrambling to transition their business models is that consumer choice has been

---

[1] Mark Savage, 'Is this the end of owing music', BBC, 3 January 2019, https://www.bbc.co.uk/news/entertainment-arts-46735093.

[2] Brad Adgate, 'Once Again, In 2023, Many Cable Networks Had A Decline in Audience', *Forbes*, 3 January 2024, https://www.forbes.com/sites/bradadgate/2024/01/03/once-again-in-2023-many-cable-networks-had-a-decline-in-audience/?sh=289207bd3d92.

Defining a Startup Mindset 3

a moving target in the last five years due to the market becoming oversaturated with content that ad dollars get poured into Google, Facebook, and other platforms where consumers could be reached.

The newspaper industry, despite being a legacy industry that enjoyed unrivalled success in the years prior to online news publications, is struggling to keep up with digital news. So much so that print editions are a novelty because news is read primarily on the phone. Print manuscripts lack the convenience and ease of access. Many independent news outlets rely on donations and making sure current subscribers continue their loyalty. In an interview with Leezel Tanglao, a senior editor for membership and innovation with the *HuffPost*, she mentioned that she analyses ways to innovate and engage with *HuffPost* readers in a time when print newspapers are suffering a decline.

Our world has gone digital in every way possible and it is vital that companies continue to create product enhancements before a new entrant in the market makes things change. Last year, we saw the instant rise and fall of Quibi, a streaming platform designed for ten-minute video series. With over one hundred million in funding, it never existed more than a year before tumbling. One of the reasons was that providing a three-month free trial period did not compete well enough with the other options that consumers gravitated towards.

Recently, Gary Vaynerchuk, social media connoisseur and entrepreneur, had a conversation that TikTok is currently what MTV was in the 1980s.[3] The way content is demanded and consumed has been vastly altered into short-form videos that are entertaining and engaging, to say the least. Tik Tok's impact cannot be immediately measured but it goes to show that one app can change the way people spend their time and that is a core benefit of technology.

---

[3] https://youtu.be/ITTiCqC8lnI.

As the age of technology has arrived on the red carpet that is the internet, regular people around the world are being drawn into the phenomenon that is TikTok and ditching cable TV for a platform that appeals to their tastes in a tailored way.

Smartphones and apps (digital products) have changed lifestyles exponentially. It feels like modes of accomplishing things like communication and shopping are efforts of convenience that free up time to be spent on the internet. While consumers have gone digital, in-person experiences are being reconstructed. The idea of going to the mall, convenience store, or grocery store is becoming an afterthought with the option of Amazon, Instacart, BigBasket, and an almost frictionless experience that top brands are providing with the help of Shopify and Instagram shopping to name a few.

Businesses around the world are at the mercy of knowing how to keep up with new trends and make sure they remain competitive because any day, a new idea can come out and rupture existing businesses. This may mean a hyperemphasized approach to UI/UX design or product features that encourage a purchase instead of just being informational. The success and mass adoption of technology products at scale is democratizing access to, well, everything, and creating new modes of doing day-to-day tasks.

And then came Covid-19. March of 2020 saw an unprecedented change in the US and across the globe. State and local governments mandated shelter in place instructions for the country due to Covid-19. Drastically, millions of people were forced to stay at home unless they fit the essential workers' category. To make matters worse, about thirty million people lost their jobs and became unemployed, catalysing fiscal stimulus aid and government intervention. Many small and large business owners were forced to shut their doors due to government-imposed social distancing efforts. Restaurant owners across the country and in Dan's hometown, San Francisco, especially, were forced to figure out how to accommodate diners while operating as take-out-only businesses.

Have legacy industries such as travel, hospitality, and food reinvented their mindsets towards business to serve the present reality? Simply put, there is no turning back from the age of digital transformation. This new order has affected corporations at all levels, forcing rapid change and a fight for survival. Never before has having a digital aspect and mindset been so relevant to brick-and-mortar businesses. What exists is a constant tug of war that corporate executives face daily—continue what has made the company successful in the first place or adopt a digital mindset and technologies that are presumed to enhance the overall business?

As the route to building great software-based products is well documented, the appetite to transform products into companies is rising meteorically. Everyone knows that Facebook started in a Harvard dorm room or that Google started in a Palo Alto garage. Zoom, a video communications platform, quickly rose in popularity during Covid-19, becoming the number one app downloaded on the App Store and growing its user base from twenty million to three hundred million in just a span of a few weeks. This reinforced the fact that businesses need to adapt quickly. That is the essence of today's digital age and our main preoccupation. New agile ideas entering the market and changing consumer behaviour.

Do you want to start your own business? Maybe a better question would be: Are there problems that need a solution you see yourself being a part of? We think that the idea behind being an entrepreneur is more mainstream today than ever before. The millennial and Gen Z generations grew up watching their parents work nine to five for twenty years and spend most of their time in an office. But 2020 ushered in a new era of remote work enabling workers the freedom to work from home. As people can work from home and make a decent living, their time gets freed up for million-dollar ideas. They finally have the space to ask themselves: Why can't my ideas for a startup turn into reality?

If we want to thrive and encounter fewer hurdles it is critical that we respond in work and life with attitudes that embrace change and challenges so that we can enjoy success. It is time organizations and aspiring startup founders reflect on the way they operate to flourish in times of uncertainty.

This is where we need to adopt a Startup Mindset.

According to *The Merriam-Webster Dictionary*, a mindset is defined as 'a mental attitude or inclination'. Many of us have been conditioned to think a certain way and operate based on principles that might be appropriate for a certain time and place in the past. Getting into modern psychology, mindsets are what dictate our actions. Mindsets are composed of feelings and the baggage of past events because humans are the only species to process information.

The past decade has already altered our daily habits both socially and personally. Our phones dictate most of our decisions to some extent while the outside world is also soon to be altered with the rise of driverless cars, permanent work from home settings, online dating, the list goes on and on. Today's world requires us to question our old ways of thinking as a rapid pace of change is already a norm and the predictable ways of the past do not exist any more. According to Steve Blank, an entrepreneurship professor at both Stanford and Berkeley, 'A startup is a temporary organisation designed to search for a repeatable and scalable business model.'[4] What distinguishes a startup company from a regular small and medium enterprise is the ambition of the company to scale, and this scale is mostly achieved through advancements in science and technology.

Thus, this book challenges us to reflect on our existing mindsets that were inculcated in us in the past. Founders of highly successful startups in the Silicon Valley have developed an effective mindset over the decades, which can be applied to both

---

[4] Kevin Ready, 'A Startup Conversation with Steve Blank', *Forbes*, 28 August 2012, https://www.forbes.com/sites/kevinready/2012/08/28/a-startup-conversation-with-steve-blank/?sh=27a4f95cf0db.

Defining a Startup Mindset

aspiring technology founders or innovators and also those who don't necessarily want to be a founder but want to ramp up their careers. These startup mindsets are integral towards scaling the type of impact we want to see in our lifetimes.

The core characteristics of a startup mindset are:

1. **Balancing a changing landscape while staying true to core values**
    As the world is changing rapidly, the pressures on each of us increase exponentially as well. Within this chaos many make decisions that might not be aligned with what you believe and how you think the world should work. Like a startup, every day is a chance to increase the probability of success or to navigate a landmine that can shut down your business and your dream forever. This state of constant chaos is normal in new ventures, where uncertainty is at its maximum, and the chances for survival are at their lowest. One thing that can distinguish good founders from great founders is the hyper-consistency in the mission and the values of why the firm was built in the first place. The mindset of being able to constantly balance change and chaos but focusing on the North Star is so important.

    When we spoke to hundreds of founders in the podcast, we asked each one of them if the companies they have created had many 'near-death experiences' and most said that they had several. Whether it be running out of money in the bank or having a regulatory license blocking the launch or a venture investor who committed but pulled out at the last minute, there are so many chances a company can fail. If you don't have this mindset of mission first, a normal person would give up at step 1. What keeps a startup alive despite this set of landmines is the relentless focus on the pursuit of change, which can be attributed to the team, and company they have built could have a chance to actually create the change they envisioned to create when they started the company with an idea and a dream.

2. **Staying relentless and resilient**

As a society we have a perception of success as only achievements, milestones, or events worth talking about. However, all the countless late nights and sacrifices that go into a ten-year success need to be spoken about as well. There are people going into their one hundredth interview hoping to receive an offer, founders pitching to their hundredth investor or customer, an author revising their work for the hundredth time, someone fixing their website, filming a video for Tik Tok all for more than just the first time. But we naturally get impatient and lose interest when our efforts do not bring us the objective we set out to achieve.

On an episode of Netflix's hit TV Show *Cobra Kai*, one of the main characters, Daniel LaRusso, says his route in life has been circular and never a straight line. An entrepreneurial pursuit will lead you to rejections and you might have to reassess many decisions. If one wants to be a successful entrepreneur, they'll need to relentlessly pursue the next customer, hire, investor, and may feel as if they are going in circles but will hit their goal when they don't necessarily expect it. This is what success looks like beyond the surface. To shine in the brightest moments, we have to work when it does not look pretty, embrace setbacks, dead ends, and not just the desired outcome.

3. Pushing your personal boundaries

In an interview we did with René Morkos, founder of the AI construction startup ALICE Technologies, he recalled playing with little cut-outs of paper and shuffling them around on a table to mimic algorithms before writing some code and developing an algorithm. ALICE is a generative construction simulator that builds a construction project for you in millions of different ways. René says this is the fastest and cheapest way to do so. When things are delayed due to the weather or whatever reason, you can input the changes and receive the best ways to move forward.

In April 2024 alone, more than USD 2 trillion were poured into construction projects in the United States.[5]

Prior to starting ALICE, René worked as a civilian contractor in Afghanistan managing 114 people and helped construct a cruise ship terminal in Amsterdam, the Netherlands. He gained first-hand experience with the problems of the industry such as scheduling issues and mismanagement of steps.

He then created ALICE from the standpoint of solving these problems with the software he built. René was able to apply new technology to enhance an existing industry lacking this type of tool. While an outsider may just look at the highlights and what's available in press releases, building ALICE was no easy task as he recalls clocking twenty and half hours a day, putting everything he had into what he was doing. The whole point was to find moments where he would break.

As he was working on ALICE, he started solving real problems and recalled showing the algorithm to a guy at

---

[5] United States Census Bureau, 'Monthly Construction Spending, May 2024', https://www.census.gov/construction/c30/current/index.html.

a job site who said it worked. Moreover, ALICE won first place in a competition for the best product coming out of Stanford.

To date, ALICE has raised USD 43 million[6] from venture capitalists and René remembers being rejected 300 times before hearing one yes in the early days.

What was present in René's mindset was an obsession with solving a problem for prospective customers, and if you do something for 15,000 hours you're going to fall in love with it.

For René, operating with a startup mindset involved pushing his personal boundaries and inventing a product that has the ability to address problems at scale. In emphasizing doing the work for the right personal and external reasons, one has a greater purpose than just being motivated by money, fame, or self-perceived success. When we work towards a vision of the future that excites us and provides value to others in novel ways, we teeter on the precipice of impactful contributions and outsized returns.

The future is upon us and operating with a startup mindset is key to making sure organizations remain competitive and afloat. Software sales of prominent tech companies increase year on year and quarter on quarter primarily due to the big markets and their market expansion strategies, and with the core value of their technology solving pain points and making the lives of digital businesses easier, we are marching towards a digital innovation-driven economy.

---

[6] ALICE Technologies, 'ALICE Technologies Extends Funding Series B Round to Access $47M in Capital', PR Newswire, 11 April 2023, https://www.prnewswire.com/news-releases/alice-technologies-extends-funding-series-b-round-to-access-47m-in-capital-301793474.html.

2

Startup Mindset versus Traditional Business Mindset

'If you want something you have never had, you must be willing to do something you have never done.'

—Thomas Jefferson

There are many misconceptions, even within the business community, about what is a startup. Because of the popularity and mystique of starting up a company today versus even ten years ago, it seems that many businesses call themselves a startup. One thing to realize though is that there is a very logical way to understand what a startup business means versus focusing on traditional businesses. Given that a startup aims to create exponential scale in the long-term, it is inherently biased towards taking higher risk earlier on in order to achieve fast growth later on in the life cycle of the company. For example, Uber, despite being a public company already, announced in the beginning of 2023 that it has made a profit after fifteen years.[7] But why is it that even for the many years that company was unprofitable, the valuation of

---

[7] Jessica Bursztynsky, 'Uber just posted its first annual profit as a public company', Fast Company, 2 July 2024, https://www.fastcompany.com/91025396/uber-just-posted-its-first-annual-profit-as-a-public-company.

the company was still sustained at billions of dollars? The answer lies truly in the potential for growth and the amount of time it can take to achieve this growth.

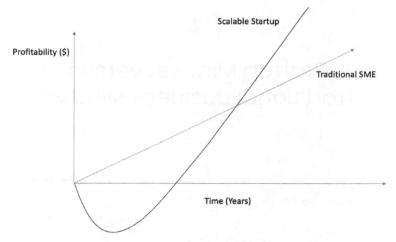

The contrast between a scalable startup versus a traditional SME

A startup is a business in which the expectations of growth rate, long-term profitability, and scale are compressed into a shorter amount of time. For example, when a new company takes on its first formal venture capital funding, an investment round occurs where a professional fund manager decides to invest in these early startups, typically after the company demonstrates a working product and some initial customer traction.

The expectation after this funding round, often called seed round, is to reach USD 1 million annual recurring run rate or reach about USD 80,000 to 100,000 recurring monthly revenue within eighteen months or less. The growth rates that can be expected at this stage could be 10 to 15 per cent per month. Most businesses aspire to even have a growth rate of 15 per cent per year but these scalable companies have outsized expectations to achieve this growth rate in a month.

For traditional businesses, instead of looking for a high risk–high reward outcome, a small business enterprise (SME) or traditional business optimizes for predictability in the long run. For example, a traditional services company like a consulting firm or training firm can predict what the revenue and margin per employee deployed into a specific account might be. It could be constrained, however, by the number of staff they can hire and how much clients are willing to pay them at a price above their cost. Even if, for example, a client wants to hire three thousand consultants in the next seven days, the growth of the company might not be able to service that demand right away with a quality that is needed. An alternative scalable path could be if that same services company can create a consulting AI bot so clients can be serviced even if the human consultant is working on six or eight concurrent customer services without having to hire and deploy more people to clients.

While it might seem that we are alluding to a traditional business not being the right path or perhaps being 'stuck in the old ways', this is far from what could be the truth. Many businesses that could be bucketed in these traditional business models are some of the most profitable and predictable businesses that anyone can start and even become millionaires or billionaires. For example, fast-food companies like McDonald's were worth over USD 200 billion[8] in February 2024, and a Filipino competitor Jollibee was worth over USD 5 billion.[9] Most entrepreneurs will likely succeed more in this type of business and most investors will understand the economics and business models of these kinds of ventures. One must ask honestly: Do you have skills and mindset to attempt to start a scalable startup venture, or are you more comfortable with a highly predictable model that a traditional business brings?

---

[8] 'McDonald's Corporation (MCD)', Yahoo Finance, https://finance.yahoo.com/quote/MCD/?guccounter=1.

[9] 'Jollibee Foods Corporation (JBFCF)', Yahoo Finance, https://finance.yahoo.com/quote/JBFCF/.

Digital Disruption in Traditional Businesses Is Accelerating

While traditional businesses have thrived for the past thirty to fifty years without relying much on technology, consumers are dictating which trends are hot and which aren't, meaning that there is more choice and tastes are changing. This means to serve customers best, brands must innovate within their own suite of existing products by making them more appealing and user-friendly.

TD Ameritrade, an online brokerage firm characterized by their commission-based trades noticed significant changes to their business when Robinhood, a new mobile-friendly trading and investing app with their key characteristic being commission-free trades, appealed to younger users and began absorbing market share and changing the individual investing game forever. Founders Bhaiju Bhatt and Vlad Tenev were fresh out of Stanford when they came up with the idea.

At first, TD Ameritrade, which owned the vast majority of the market share, did not even bat an eye about what Robinhood was doing. But as the months and years went by, Robinhood grew daily active users and proved that there was a market and demand among consumers to use their trading platform over their competitors'. What set Robinhood apart was their approach to democratizing the investing landscape in such a way that their product prioritized young, first-time investors. When someone first downloads the Robinhood app, the user interface is much more pleasant to use compared to TD Ameritrade's. This results in more app usage that leads to more trades and happier end users. Once TD removed commission-based trades, their amount of trade volume increased by three times.

In 2019, Charles Schwab began offering commission-free trades in an effort to bring back their user base and compete with

Robinhood. While Schwab and TD are legacy corporations, that did not stop Robinhood from building their platform. They saw the way that their competitors ran their business and believed a counterintuitive approach would lead to success within their own startup.

The economy thrives because of the digital shift and businesses without the ability to adopt an in-house approach to innovation get left behind. As soon as Google's self-driving car unit, Waymo, started working on a digital fleet that would render the need for human-driven vehicles unnecessary, General Motors took notice. They saw that their legacy industry could be severely affected if they could not produce their own cars with self-driving capabilities. The company had to act fast and choose their options: continue their traditional manufacturing operations and not adopt a self-driving car research and development division or look outward to remain competitive in the future.

In 2017, General Motors' CEO Dan Ammann announced its purchase of self-driving car startup, Cruise. Suddenly, GM had gone from fears of losing the race to autonomous vehicles thus avoiding losing millions in sales down the line to leading the charge towards an autonomous car future.

In the fashion industry in 2020, clothing sales were down 79 per cent in the months of April and May in the US but sales of Stitch Fix, an e-commerce platform that curates styles for its customers in a subscription box model, were only down 9 per cent.[10] Stitch Fix benefited from the Covid-19 economy, which rewarded businesses with a 'startup and digital presence'

---

[10] Jeff Cox, 'Retail sales plunge a record 16.4% in April, far worse than predicted', CNBC, 15 May 2020, https://www.cnbc.com/2020/05/15/us-retail-sales-april-2020.html.

Lauren Thomas, 'Stitch Fix sales fell 9% as coronavirus delayed orders, sees sales growth ahead as backlog clears', CNBC, 8 June 2020, https://www.cnbc.com/2020/06/08/stitch-fix-sfix-reports-fiscal-q3-2020-net-loss.html.

that use solutions driven by innovation, drive consumer demand, and usurp traditional ways of commerce.

If the last decade has taught us anything, it is that the appetite for innovation, disruption, and change are driven by the startup mindset of being prepared to be a prime player in legacy industries combined with digital enhancements.

3

Developing Your Startup Mindset

'I'll do whatever it takes to win games, whether it's sitting on a bench waving a towel, handing a cup of water to a teammate, or hitting the game-winning shot.'

—Kobe Bryant

One day, Ronald Ro walked into his newborn daughter's bedroom and picked her up from her crib to notice Ella had developed some pretty serious eczema on her fingers. Troubled as any parent would be, Ron wanted to find out what its cause was. He didn't grow up with eczema, so he wondered why his daughter had it. Could it be an allergic reaction to food or a hereditary condition?

The doctor ruled that neither was the culprit. Coincidently, a good friend of his, Kevin Cho, noticed his daughter had asthma around the same time. The pair, unsure of what the underlying causes for both the conditions were, decided to do some research. They realized that they needed to ensure safe and healthy environments at home, and this meant having a basic understanding of what elements in the house might be leading a newborn child to develop eczema and asthma. Upon doing some research they discovered that invisible factors like dust mites and air quality have more to do with eczema and asthma than

18   Startup Mindsets

they thought. For instance, volatile organic compounds and high humidity lead to respiratory reactions and skin irritation.

Understanding that humidifiers and purifiers would only do so much, they wanted more data about what was happening around them so they could arrive at the right solution. Ron started by putting a few sensors in a hardware component together as a prototype. Using his expertise in mechanical engineering, he was able to create a device that did the bare minimum of reading particulate elements. Temperature, humidity, and PM 2.5, which measures atmospheric particulate matter smaller than 2.5 microns, were important to track because volatile organic compounds can cause skin and respiratory irritation. So, they found a way to measure these amounts by putting together their first air quality monitor.

Ron's wife, Jeongkat, encouraged him to make it a tangible product. She said, 'Why don't you at least do a moonlight project or something if you can? Just know I don't want to live with you hearing all these complaints like you couldn't do it because of family or something.'

A familial support system was the green light he needed to start executing. After all, the problem might never have been identified had Ella not had allergies.

As we'll learn, mindsets are not constant, they need to be reinforced by the people and circumstances around you. Because emotions are fleeting, one minute you want to solve health issues caused by polluted air then the next you have doubts. Having a community of individuals that supports what you're doing provides the emotional validation we crave.

In Ron's case, the supporting cast really helped him emotionally to overcome the struggles of the day-to-day process.

Fast-forward a few months, the pair created a device to measure indoor air quality that is now known as Awair. You can find their devices in homes, offices, and hospitals across the country providing accurate insights on the air we breathe and the health concerns that may stem from poor air quality in closed spaces. Awair was not built overnight and took many iterations and venture dollars to build a minimum viable product along with coaching during their time in Techstars and StartX accelerators.

Ron and Kevin could have just sat there and let someone else solve their problems but there is power in the freedom of solving a problem that makes people's lives better. When one takes control of their situation and refuses to succumb to the world's existing answers because they're not good enough, a mission is born. Being an entrepreneur starts with which problems are worth building a solution for.

Awair devices now sit in the homes of thousands of people, providing peace of mind and clarity over indoor environments with suggestions like buying houseplants or cracking a window open to alert people on how to breathe better. When the 2020 California wildfires were out of control during the months of August and September, sparking a record twenty-eight days of spare air alerts, Dan purchased an Awair Element, the company's flagship product. Once he plugged the device into his bedroom socket, he was shocked to have received a score of 63 out of 100. This meant that the air in his room was polluted. The metric that measures smoke, PM 2.5, was red in the hundreds while other metrics like CO_2 and humidity were also displayed on Dan's smartphone. He then realized the true value of the product and how important it was to know what the air quality was to make the proper adjustments.

To date, Awair has raised USD 21 million with investments from Emerson and Techstars to name a few. An Awair device is located on Dan's nightstand in his bedroom and helps him breathe easier.

Ron used his skills and unique background to create a better life for his family. He often recalls that many times throughout the journey, he wanted to give up, but credits his kids as the support system that helped him keep going. While admitting he is still in the thick of the journey and struggling every day, he pushed through many failures and nights of hard work for his family and the idea of granting more peace of mind to other families and employees who could use the peace of mind that comes with knowing the air we breathe doesn't cause any harm.

Some people become founders by chance, others are born with the entrepreneurial spirit, inherit it from their family, or grow up in environments that force them to hustle. In our experience, there is no prerequisite for starting a company, it is literally just filing the paperwork to incorporate the entity. The real work comes in with having what it takes to scale a business and making enough income from the revenue to afford your living expenses.

The market does not care much about aesthetics behind the creators of products and services. Create a good enough solution to a pesky problem, whether it enhances value or reduces friction for the customer at scale, and you are off to a great start. But what enables some to make the leap while others prefer a stable job, the nine-to-five majority the workforce is composed of? We wondered about this question while writing this book. And it has to do with having a startup mindset. After interviewing more than a hundred entrepreneurs what made them start their businesses, a common theme was this belief that there was something more.

When Dan asked John Green, CEO of Nada, what gave him the belief to create a real estate investment platform that lets people invest in city funds—think of Exchange Traded Funds (ETF) but for the real estate in cities; city funds unlock the home equity market for both homeowners and real estate investors—he told Dan, 'At the end of the day, if you fundamentally believe that the products you're building should exist in the market and that they do create value for people, then everything else becomes white noise.'

Prior to launching a product or service, there is no 100 per cent way to know that it will be a massive success, but believing

Developing Your Startup Mindset

that it benefits people makes it more saleable and desirable to work on no matter what stage the company is in.

All forms of entrepreneurship revolve around a notion of providing some sort of access to a product or service but startups, in particular, couple engineering talent to create innovative products and services that are only as good as the way the market consumes that technology. Running a startup involves a lot of risks whether it is the obvious financial pressure or emotional drawback that come with the day-to-day grind. There is the ubiquitous presence of weighing the notion that this can fail versus the guarantee a stable profession provides. For those who dare to build something that can stand on its own through hard work, it is vital to examine one's energy levels and commitment; think long and hard about how ideas can gain validation and have proof of concept.

Making the Ultimate Decision: Staying in Corporate versus Starting Up

Every year in January, Earl, one of the main startup advisers in the Philippines, always gets asked for advice by a number of corporate friends who share their aspirations to 'leave the nine to five' and 'be their own boss'. Many have told him that they want to be the next Elon Musk or Mark Zuckerberg and they feel that this is the right time for them to go all in and leave the comforts of a steady pay cheque.

An investor and a fellow founder himself, as much as he laces many mentorship sessions like these with much optimism and encouragement, he also balances them out with doses of reality that entrepreneurship is not going to get you more time to hang out at the beach drinking fruity beverages, but it will demand much more of you than any job that you'll have in your life. This is especially true, since most venture capital firms, even at the pre-seed stage, require a full-time commitment from their founders.

Would you really do anything and give up everything to the point that it affects your lifestyle? Is the challenge you're facing important to you? Now, this is all a matter of selection and opinion but the startup world tends to test limits and this is not always the case for your average founder. That's how much love and attention an early-stage startup requires.

Some context here: Earl was a late bloomer as a founder. He decided to start a startup at the tender age of thirty-seven. This feels late for many. But in actuality, while many founders start companies in their twenties, it's not uncommon for people in their thirties and forties to become entrepreneurs. What was different for Earl was that he now had a wife and kids, and was well into his corporate life. If leaving an executive role in a financial services company wasn't enough, it was the responsibility of being the sole breadwinner in the family that raised the stakes for this decision as it was not just his life that would be affected but other individuals' too because he was ultimately responsible for their well-being.

Here are the five questions you must ask yourself before leaving the *job*:

1. **Do you have a business or just an idea?** Is there external validation that people need this? Fundamentally, are you quitting your job for a hobby or a real business opportunity? When Earl was in Cisco, the team that he was in called this the 'anyone but your mother rule'. A true test of a business is that someone is paying for your product or your service besides your mother, uncle, or friends. Again, payment is key, as it seems many people start businesses without any commercial validation, often relying on gut instinct or market surveys. The best validation is to have paying customers or, for B2B, commercial agreements to know that you have a real business opportunity worth pursuing.

2. **Are you financially prepared to take on the business?** Can your income go too close to zero for six to twelve months minimum? This is probably the toughest fact to hear. Many of us have dreams of starting a company, but we can't afford to do so. Not all of us have rich aunties or uncles, so the option of just quitting is predicated on financial savings, particularly asking if you have four to twelve months of household expenses that you have saved up. When Earl and his co-founder were starting their startup, he only had about four months of household expenses saved up before tossing in the towel, but note that it took him five years to save up that money consciously every month. He called it the personal startup bank account or a dedicated account to fund the first few months of living expenses if and when a startup idea would be so exciting that he would decide to go full-time into the journey. Why is this important? Although we see movies or articles where people get funded in a day or a week, in reality you should never assume that external funding will come, especially at the earliest stages of a company's pre-product stage. It could take months or even a year to be able to progress enough in the business that external investors will take a bet on your idea, so make sure you are prepared financially for this decision.

3. **Will you have any regrets if this business does not become successful?** According to an article by Elizabeth Pollman from the University of Pennsylvania and European Corporate Governance Institute (ECGI) in 2023, 'Approximately 75 percent of venture-backed startups fail—the number is difficult to measure, however, and by some estimates it is far greater.'[11] This doesn't even account for the millions of businesses that do *not*

---

[11] https://www.ecgi.global/sites/default/files/working_papers/documents/startupfailure.pdf.

get past the standards of venture capital. Despite these odds, most founders-to-be start companies not to solve a personal mission or a problem, but to fulfil the dream of building a unicorn and maybe retire early. The past five years have given a false sense of hope for this generation that founding a company is sexy and is the path towards millions. A critical question you must ask yourself is: Can you be happy with the fact that you have a rare chance in your lifetime to try to solve something important to you and perhaps for the world? Can you imagine that in four or five years, the company might not exist or your startup could be sold for zero dollars, but the mission would still continue?

4. **Do you and your family all know the sacrifices needed to give this a shot?** In 2014, *Inc.* magazine published an article entitled 'The Start of a Company, the End of a Marriage: Launching a business can shatter the founder's marriage.'[12] This is because the founder's life is no easy path, mired in stressful situations, near-death experiences and personal income instability that is almost impossible to shield your family from, unlike a normal job where you can 'leave your work worries at the door'. Can you have an honest discussion with your loved ones about what this decision of quitting means for them and how this will affect them individually? Earl in particular had a sit-down with his wife and two middle-school-aged kids indicating that they as a family might have to cut down a lot from their lifestyle, and that Dad would be busier and have less time for the next few years. Even if it was difficult, humility had to set in as well, and he had to ask

---

[12] Jessica Bruder, 'The Start of a Company, the End of a Marriage', *Inc.*, June 2014, https://www.inc.com/magazine201406/jessica-bruder/how-to-balance-company-and-marriage.html.

Developing Your Startup Mindset

his parents and in-laws for support as they might need to help his family during this time. If you decide to start a company, are you prepared to have these conversations with the closest people around you?

5. **Do you have an unfair advantage in building this business?** The last question is putting the investor's mind into your business. Will you trust your own money and invest in the business because you and your founders are the right people to pull this business off? Do you have unfair insights, expertise, or advantage to make this happen for the world?

If we had to sum up the advice to many, the simple answer to if people should go full-time comes down to timing. Timing of your readiness as an individual to mentally, emotionally, and financially go towards this path, and timing of the market to accept the idea that you have. Even if this seems gloomy, starting a company and seeing how it has impacted hundreds of thousands of individuals is one of the most rewarding feelings an entrepreneur can feel in their lifetime, most never regret the day they decide to pack up their suit and trade it for a startup hoodie.

4

Find One Phrase that Encapsulates Your Personal Mission

'Your purpose in life is to find your purpose and give your whole heart and soul to it.'

—Siddhartha Gautama, aka Buddha

In 2018, Earl attended the Social Innovation Summit at the Consumer Electronics Show. The organization Dear World challenged the audience to reflect on a time in their lives that changed them—a time that still had a large impact on their values and how they made life decisions. They also urged the audience to write down a phrase that they remembered the most from that specific moment. Honestly, this was one of the most powerful exercises he had in any conference, and the funny thing is, it was inside the largest technology show in the world. A very heart-centred summit in a sea of data-centred discussions.

For this one, in particular, Earl reflected on his life mission, and wrote down one phrase—'Maximizing human potential.' After thinking about it during the reflection session, the words held such a deep and meaningful mission for him, and there was one story that came up over and over in his mind as one of the pivotal experiences that have stayed in his consciousness for close to twenty years. At the risk of being vulnerable, Earl would like to share this story with you:

Since I was a young child, I was always curious about who my grandfather was. He was the patriarch of the 'Valencia family' someone who I haven't met but seems I had so much connection to. He was not from a wealthy family but from a small town called Guagua, Pampanga, about 90 kilometres from Manila. He got a scholarship to go to the civil engineering school at the University of the Philippines, the top engineering school in the country, and to make ends meet and survive the big city, he had to do janitorial work during his school years. Years after graduating, with a wife and six kids, he ended up starting a civil engineering and logging business in the southern city of Davao. He grew this business into a diversified conglomerate with over USD 50 million in revenue per year in the 50s, 60s, and 70s. According to Google, with inflation, that USD 50 million per year in 1960 would be equivalent to USD 500 million per year in 2024's worth.

After building his businesses, the same man wanted to focus his energy on the public sector and ended up becoming the Minister of Public Works and Communications of the Philippines under President Macapagal. Imagine this, from a scholar-janitor boy to holding the 'top engineering post' in the country in a lifetime. That's what getting and taking advantage of opportunities can bring someone. Unfortunately, I never met the man that all my uncles and aunties talk about so fondly. He passed away six months after I was born. Because of this, my grandmother always said I looked like my grandfather and maybe part of his spirit lives within me. I am a direct beneficiary of someone who received a life-changing opportunity and how opportunities can change the trajectories of upcoming generations.

Fast-forward to when I was sixteen, in a very different circumstance. Because of my grandfather's legacy, I grew up in what we might call a 'semi-charmed' life, with country clubs, private schools, and being raised in one of the most affluent neighbourhoods in the Philippines called Ayala Alabang. In fact, my wife now, who I grew up with, can't believe that I did not play in the streets or I thought that going on trips abroad every year was normal.

My life took a serious turn when I wanted to go to the same school and college my grandfather went to, the University of the Philippines, where, unlike his circumstances of hardship and struggle, I had the opposite experience. I had a car, an allowance, and a dorm on campus with air conditioning when the normal dorm didn't have any. I, however, had classmates from many different socio-economic classes. UP was a true meritocracy—there was an entrance test—and your percentile in the test determined which department you would be eligible for, it was called the infamous 'course quota'—the number of slots a course has the capacity to take in. For my programme, Electronics and Communications Engineering, you had to score in the top 2 per cent of the math section to qualify. That's the top 1,400 math scores out of 70,000 test-takers.

My classmates were brilliant even though they had very different circumstances from mine, and some of them shared with me that they were sons of taxi drivers and farmers. They were so smart and hardworking that they often got higher marks than I did. This was the first time that I had friends who weren't like me and my friends growing up. I remember that on weekends, I would typically go out clubbing or at least watch a movie in our high-end mall, but on Friday, when I asked some of my classmates what they will be doing during the weekend, one of them replied to my surprise and said, 'I have to work and help earn for my family.' While I thought at that time that the major decisions in my college years revolved around what to do during the weekend, some had to think of survival during those times.

As I now reflect, looking at my own personal history, I feel that some of my classmates could have been like my grandfather—first-generation scholars for whom maybe this education changed the trajectories of their families for the better. It may have been that this was the same exact circumstance of my grandfather—in the same exact school, in the same exact college, walking in the same exact footsteps—but just seventy years before I stepped foot on the same campus.

Two years after I went to college, when I spoke to my brother who went to the US, he encouraged me to apply to transfer to a US university because of the vast number of opportunities I might have if I were exposed at an early age to the latest technical research as an engineering undergrad at a major US university. I applied to around ten schools—from Princeton, Stanford, Caltech to MIT and others. After months of waiting, most schools rejected me except for two—the University of Michigan and the University of New Hampshire, both with conditional acceptances, with one school that hadn't replied yet, Boston University.

I accepted the offer to go to the University of Michigan, which had one of the top five Electrical Engineering programmes, and already chanted their famous slogan of 'Go Blue!' and couldn't wait to leave the Philippines. I thought I was home-free and because of that, I didn't really care about my own grades now in college because I was US-bound. I was overconfident and took third-year courses even though I was a second year. Because of my overconfidence, I got the first F in my life, but at that time I really didn't care.

The admissions in Michigan finally asked for my final transcript to show my final marks in sophomore year, but upon review, they informed me that I had failed to meet their minimum GPA requirement by .1 (a converted 3.4 versus a 3.5). They rescinded my conditional offer and rejected me. I was heartbroken and close to depression but continued on to my third year of school. In August, after my mid-term exam, resigned that I will have to finish my studies in Manila, I got a large envelope in the mail with an acceptance from BU. Apparently, it got lost in the mail for three months and lucky for me, when I called back they said that even if the semester will start in four weeks, I can still come. I remember my mom worrying about how to pay since they only had one year of US tuition saved up for me, but I promised, 'Just pay for the first year, and I'll get a scholarship for the rest.'

I told Dr Rowena 'Gev' Guevara, the Electrical Engineering Department Chair and a PhD graduate from the University of Michigan the good news. Because of her love for the Philippines, she came back to the country after receiving her PhD, even though she could get a tenure track faculty position anywhere. She is one of the most progressive academics I know because she transformed the department through joint initiatives with industry and elevated the stature of the programme. I was supposed to just say that I was going to transfer and go to Boston to continue my studies. I was nervous, since everybody knew she was strict, but I just thought I'd say goodbye for five minutes and let her sign my papers and go. Those five minutes turned into one hour of scolding, discussion, and lecturing.

What she said there for one hour I don't really remember, but one line has stuck with me until this day, a line that I will never forget. She said, 'Why did you take someone else's spot?' She said I could have gone to another private college that my family could afford. You see, in the Philippines, in the top ten colleges, UP was ranked #1 then #2–9 were private colleges, and #10 was a public institution. The tuition of these private colleges was around P 150,000 per year or about USD 3,000 per year. Note that the GDP per capita in the Philippines is around USD 2,950. This is why the 'rich get richer' in most emerging markets because even quality education is a privilege and not a right. She was implying that because of the limited spots they had, my slot could have gone to someone else who could have benefited more. It could have changed their life, but I chose to take the spot and, after two years, dump it.

Those words didn't just change my life, but solidified my appreciation for how education, investment, and someone 'taking a chance' on someone can change the trajectory of a human being. This is why every day I aim to figure out how to create a meritocracy in the world—that maybe I might give my spot back to that woman or man who needs it the most.

People ask why I'm so obsessed with creating impact through innovation. Why do I need to build and work for companies that aim to 'level the playing field'? We modified our selection process to take out last names and affiliations such as schools, since that could be a determinant of social status or unfair access to resources. Why I travelled every weekend, around the Philippines and Southeast Asia, to give talks to students in most public universities? This is why for years I never gave up the vision that maybe the Philippine government would catch on the innovation trend, even if people repeatedly told me that it would be a 'waste of time' dealing with the public sector. This is why I go to the World Economic Forum events to realize that there are other people who care about creating global change. Even if I am in the US, with late night or early morning calls, I still continue to advise founders and companies in the impact and innovation spaces in emerging markets. This is why my goal is that maybe in my lifetime, I'd be able to impact a billion people and help them maximize their potential.

Some people call me crazy for believing that I can make a difference. Some people call me an idealist because I think meritocracy is possible. Looking back to see how a stroke of luck and hard work gave me the opportunities I had my entire life—I see a calling, an obligation to do something, to maybe be someone. I will give back that spot not just to one person, but to millions more.

5

Dare to Be Different

Add Real Value

When Mark Zuckerberg wore the iconic shirt and a hoodie combo in 2005, that 'tech-uniform' catalysed what Facebook employees were known for. A simple shirt and zip up hoodie represented the company culture and what it meant to work for Facebook. In a sense, it meant a level of autonomy and ease of fitting in. Soon everyone from other tech companies followed suit. This simple culture set the tone for employee work ethic, it did away with fancy button ups and business casual wear. Facebook became a company that set itself apart from everyone else. Before you knew it, this attracted engineers and young hopefuls to want to join the company as employee centricity became a foundation for growth.

The 2008 financial crisis gave birth to new companies and new cultures that have paved the way for digital disruption and change among workplaces and personal habits. Most of the best companies in the world are technology companies that thrive on innovation and the ability to hone that in the marketplace.

Allbirds, a popular shoe characterized by its simplicity and ability to stand out yet fit in, crashed the startup fashion scene in 2016. A year into launch and the shoe became a tech industry fashion symbol. Everywhere from Google to startups, Allbirds became a hit and widely worn shoe among tech workers. The wool runners were seen on Larry Page, Alphabet's CEO, and Marc Andreessen, partner at venture capital firm Andreessen Horowitz, aka a16z.

Dan first saw the shoe in September of 2016 when his college roommate, Jovanni, walked out of his room and said, 'Hey, Dan, like my shoes? They're the new tech shoes, bro.' He was somewhat perplexed and didn't know how to react. At the time, he was not a fan of tech startups because of San Francisco's gentrification due to the growing presence of tech in the city. He was dismissive of anything that had to do with startups, so he turned a blind eye to Allbirds.

But he questioned how Jovanni had discovered a trend like that and refused to believe there could ever be such a thing. *A tech shoe?* he thought. What would make a shoe with no noticeable logo or fancy feature become a fashion staple for Silicon Valley dress? After all, they were at UC Riverside where the fashion sense was skewed to big brands like Nike and Adidas.

Fast-forward to when he moved back to the Bay Area after college, everyone was wearing Allbirds. He'd go on BART (Bay Area Rapid Transit) and see scores of people who also happened to be carrying a backpack repping their employer's logo, generally a tech company, wearing a set of Allbirds. It was apparent, the wool runner's popularity caught on like wildfire. As a 'startup', how did Allbirds get so popular so quickly? There's nothing crazy, extravagant or noteworthy about the shoe from a style perspective. They're the most simple shoes lacking any defining characteristics outside their simplicity and slipper-like feel. He finally succumbed to the craze and bought his first pair of navy blue wool runners in 2019, a purchase he does not regret.

What sets Allbirds apart is the fact that they combine environmentalism and sustainability with a super wearable, fashion savvy product. On top of being extremely comfortable, their shoes are made of FCC ethically and sustainably sourced

Dare to Be Different

materials such as wool from sheep sourced from ZQ Natural fibres, a nod to the founder Tim Brown's New Zealand roots.

They also developed sweet foam made out of Brazilian sugarcane and shared the groundbreaking technology with as many other shoe developers as they could. In doing so, Allbirds' embrace of their competition while standing by their mission of eco-friendly sourced materials helped them to continue to disrupt the sneaker industry at scale. The success of Allbirds comes from focusing on good design, ensuring good customer experience, and most of all focusing on the long-term vision.

Startups must be willing to do something different or what investors often refer to as 'secret sauce'. It gives them an edge over competitors that make owning equity enticing. Unique products have the ability to enhance the user experience. Brown recalls six years of listening to customer feedback and filtering out such feedback through their three non-negotiable pillars: comfort, simple design, and sustainability. If product suggestions did not make it through this filter, then the company did not implement it. What's impressive is that a young company knew how to best filter such feedback while maintaining operational discipline and championing customer centricity.

Therefore, anticipate your customer's or client's needs and work to address them in a meaningful way. The best way to do this is to get inside your client's head.

Solve Real Problems

In 1882, Thomas Edison recruited a man named Nikola Tesla to assist with a project dealing with direct currents. What became known as the electrical power grids that the United States relies on today came from these two men.

Nikola Tesla, some believe, is the true inventor of the alternate current that uses a transformer for a more efficient and less expensive system that directly competes with Edison's realization.

Thomas Edison grew jealous of the success Tesla had and made last-ditch efforts to sabotage him.

Nearly 80 per cent of the technology used in the world today comes from Nikola Tesla's inventions. What is sad, however, is that Tesla died close to bankruptcy because of the opposition he faced from John Paul Morgan and Thomas Edison monetizing his patents. It is important to be just as good of a marketer, salesman, and capitalist when it comes to applying innovation to business ventures. Although Tesla is responsible for creating life-changing inventions and products, it is doubtful if he reaped the benefits worthy of someone with such an influence.

* * *

Lots of pitch decks presented for funding/advice will have a slide or two dedicated to the problem the startup is trying to solve. These problems can range from real tangible problems for the day-to-day consumer or be heavily directed in B2B cases aimed at enterprises. There is no limit or requirement for what real-world challenges someone may want to solve because all that's needed is a real-life use case and innovation can fill the cup.

For instance, a startup had pitched us a solution to extinguishing fires with drones. We thought it was a great idea, since fires are a hazard that puts lives in danger. However, the problem was not commercial enough. As a venture capitalist, problems that have a prevalent side to them are able to hang in a long due diligence process. It was not that we did not want to help firefighters or this startup solve burning buildings, but we cannot commit a few hundred thousand dollars of fund capital on deals that do not have the potential to return the entire fund.

Ask yourself, is the problem I am providing a solution for experienced by say 10,000 people on a regular basis? If it is, both sides of the table will want to engage. This is not to say that a drone firefighter startup won't make it anywhere but the

Dare to Be Different 37

likelihood of how commercial a product can become in the future is what takes the cake.

In 2015, Dan had an idea for an app that would tell you where the best and cheapest gas was in relation to your location. It would give you points whenever you used a card towards your next fill-up. Sounds interesting, right? Well, a company called Gasbuddy already did this and it's not going to do much other than save a couple of dollars on transportation costs annually. Ideas need to be big.

What VCs and angel investors care about, for the most part, is what your company does and how it makes money. Specifically, are the markets for your solution big enough and capable of generating USD 100 million in revenue to justify their investment? How many customers and years would it take to reach such numbers? Problems vary by geography and demographic, solutions can come in the form of enhancement, promising convenience, and cost as well as time savings. VCs consider all of that and you should too.

Be a Real Innovator

Upon returning from serving a term in Afghanistan at the start of the pandemic in May 2020, Jordan Sun was back in his hometown San Jose, California. He had a decision to make: become the city of Silicon Valley's chief innovation officer in a time of pandemic crisis and take a pay cut, or accept a more lucrative job in the private sector. In Afghanistan, Jordan felt deep inside him a nagging feeling that it was time to go back to his roots and give back. He recalls not being able to fall asleep at night thinking about the pains of the city's residents, 'It reached a boiling point.' After careful consideration, Jordan accepted the city's request with the tall task of improving its residents' livelihoods, opportunities, and city experience.

San Jose had been bearing the brunt of the digital divide with a majority of the students incurring a compromise to their education because of the lack of devices for at-home instruction. The Mayor's Office of Tech and Innovation has pioneered innovative public–private partnership models to bridge the digital divide, to deploy 5G small cell networks equitably across the city, and to pilot emerging technologies, such as autonomous vehicles. 'Our objective is to build a safe, inclusive, user-friendly, sustainable city.'

A few of San Jose's pressing problems spurred by the coronavirus were making sure students in the city's school district had the right equipment to be online learners. Lockdowns prevented San Jose Unified School District from allowing in-person instruction. This meant thousands of students were forced to be educated over Zoom. Sadly, the city was facing an uphill battle in making sure that students, especially in underserved communities, had iPads, laptops, and devices that allowed for e-learning to take place at home in addition to internet access.

It's been documented that students in the community were going to Burger King to use publicly accessible Wi-Fi to do homework. The city quickly realized that there were 67,000 students without access to the internet or a device and needed to move quickly to bridge the digital divide.[13] Because Covid-19 forced classrooms to go 100 per cent remote, school administrators were left scrambling on how to teach students who lacked devices and more or less access to the internet.

Jordan's day to day included supporting projects of digital inclusion where no resident was left behind in the digital revolution

---

[13] Spotify, *Startup Mindsets* Podcast episode 'Chief Innovation Officer of San Jose - Jordan Sun', November 2020, https://open.spotify.com/episode/7zKwrvwVXVrC65PFnlp31G?si= b89b832418c14f59.

City of San Jose, 'San Jose Named Most Innovative City in the U.S.', 10 November 2020, https://www.sanjoseca.gov/Home/Components/News/News/2086/4699.

and connecting 100,000 residents in San Jose who were under- or unconnected to broadband internet. Another core project was rapidly bringing opportunistic technologies to address the community's immediate crises such as looking at tech solutions to support the small- and medium-sized businesses and prevent further job losses.

Once the Mayor's Office of Tech and Innovation developed a roadmap that involved partnering with telecommunication companies, the city saw the device count drop from 87,000 kids without a device or internet access to 13,000. It's important to delineate between crisis response action and consensus-driven action. As many citizens in the city were experiencing the crisis first-hand due to Covid-19, a positive was that the crisis was leveraged as an opportunity that shortened the digital divide.

San Jose earned the award for the most innovative city of 2020. What Jordan shared with us shows the power of vision and will of the city to use innovation in order to serve the most underserved in the community. Many of us have access to digital tools already but this shows that with the right expertise and support from the top, it could be possible to create these important changes despite the inertia and bureaucracy of a government agency or city. This also shows that a startup mindset does not only apply to small, nimble startups or large companies but it can also be applied to the public sector as well, where the most impact and innovation can be felt by a larger number of people.

6

Map Out Your Career Portfolio

'I have not failed. I've just found 10,000 ways that won't work.'
—Thomas Edison

'What do you do?' After the question 'Where you are from?' the profession-oriented question is the most common question in any networking session, although most of us, including myself, have a hard time answering this—not because we don't have an answer, but the different versions of how to answer it that justifies our current professional reality but because most of us in this new digital century do not just have one professional job, but one, two, or three different gigs that we are concurrently juggling. At the same time, a lot of us don't want the 'job' to define us as a human being, but we want to be seen as a person with passions well beyond the job alone. Earl himself has different dimensions to himself—a managing director at a large financial services firm, a husband and father of two boys, a venture adviser to impact enterprises, a social innovator, and an aspiring author and blogger.

Simon Alexander Ong, a former UK Life Coach of the Year (2019), says to never respond with a title but an action. The reason being it often connotes a judgment and preconceived notion of who you are despite just saying one word.

Imagine you came up to someone and they said they're an accountant. Now, you could be a really cool accountant with a cool personality but this often starts the conversation into the rabbit hole of interrogations or the person may not find it interesting. In a story Simon told about someone responding to the 'what do you do' question, the person said, 'I have been saving the world from boredom since before you were born.'

The other person's eyes lit up and replied, 'Tell me more.'

It is in embracing our personal stories that we are able to tell them in a way that delights and excites those listening. One of Dan's favourite quotes by Emily Dickinson is, 'Tell all the truth but tell it slant.' In the midst of running a business, one will encounter setbacks and challenges, instead of letting these struggles dictate our perception of ourselves as someone who struggles with a business, we have to choose to display a character that embodies positivity so that those we are trying to influence can see the optimism of potentially working with us.

Picture yourself pitching potential investors in your company, without the confidence because you're worried about the business growing. You won't be able to relay the optimism of the future you can create with this mindset. Instead, highlight the recent successes and emphasize why you're capable of growing the business with their assistance.

Meanwhile, you know the company is running out of cash and struggling to make revenue despite having some success and product validation.

As an entrepreneur, your career will host a hodgepodge of skills and experiences. Some that aren't your natural skill set even.

A saying that Earl's parents used to tell him when he was a child is, 'Do not be a jack of all trades and a master of none.' For the longest time, he has been giving career talks to professionals young and old. He always gets asked about his opinion on the part-time job, the extra work, or what is now called the 'side hustle'.

This somewhat controversial topic lingers in people's minds not because people don't do it—in fact, according to Bankrate.com, about four out of ten Americans are engaged in one—but because of the way society frowns upon folks who do not focus or specialize in one thing alone. Why was our mind primed to be ashamed or shame people who work eight to ten hours a day, then work an extra four to six hours on another passion project? His theory is that current society's norm is based on the old industrial revolution, where highly specialized skills were how people defined themselves day in and day out, and that long hours prevented people from doing something else besides family and work. Another theory of his is the way that middle-class societies force people to the median so that folks don't 'mess it up for everyone', people must try to gravitate towards the average.

The new digital century that we all live in now requires a different kind of mindset—one that embraces variety versus specialization, the connector rather than the vertical, the one that can simplify and deal with complexity rather than run away from it. The new leaders who grew up in the digital world should and must be able to learn new disciplines quickly and to be able to draw from a very diverse and rich experience set to tackle problems that interrelate with each other. His current role is a good example of this. He is currently in a new role that is called the digital catalyst role—a new job that needs to be part ambassador, part technology and venture capitalist, and part strategy consultant, where you need to tie in your people skills to understand the problems of the business, apply strategic frameworks, bring in best practices from other industries, and apply new technologies to solve the problems of the business. This type of interdisciplinary roles will just continue to grow in demand and accelerate over the next decade and it is important to grow leaders who can thrive in these types of 'connector' roles that never existed before as companies grapple with the new realities that technology disruptions could bring.

For this, he gives a framework to explore your career portfolio, and his advice is to have something at every box of this quadrant at any given time in your career and evaluate every year if this is still the right mix for you.

Map of a Career Portfolio in 4 Quadrants

1. **The Safe Choice** – Most of us are here, and some of us will even stay here forever. This is what you have prepared for in college or even when you were young. You default to previous experience and past situations to make decisions at work and to decide if you want to accept the work. This is what our parents call 'the stable path'. This is why a lot of friends of ours are doctors, lawyers, engineers, and healthcare professionals even if some don't really want it. The goal here is to hone your craft to make sure that you don't become obsolete soon.

2. **The Logical Progression** – This is where you build upon your skills and do something close to it. Maybe it's going to take a graduate degree to increase your pay, or maybe it's to take more responsibility in the same department in order to succeed, or even at the fundamental student level, maybe if someone was good in biology in high

school, maybe it makes sense to encourage them to go to med school or sciences.

3. **The Stretch Goal** – This is the current evening and weekend hustle. They are areas that you see today that you aren't an expert in that you would like to learn and explore. Some might want to try out a new career path, like our friends who might be engineers in the day, but financial planners at night, or someone who is an engineer in the morning and public speaker at nights and weekends. This could be owning a restaurant, kiosk, or e-commerce store and doing it part-time. This is the one that people might be willing to pay you in the short-term as well. The goal of this quadrant is to be able to learn new skills and get exposed to new thinking.

4. **The What-if Scenario** – This is what he calls the career moonshot or career trajectory game-changers. What does he mean by that? It's placing your bets on a future that might be coming and being ready for it. A good example of this is starting an entrepreneurial venture on the side for areas that you feel passionate about but not sure if it will pan out. Our opinion is to try to test out your hypothesis before shifting the buckets. This quadrant could be the basis of a brand new career for you.

If the goal is to create a portfolio, it is important that you strive to have an answer to each of the quadrants at every single point of your career and evaluate them probably every six months. So, we are challenging the readers of this note today, what is your career portfolio looking like? The next time someone asks you, 'What do you do?', don't be ashamed to say four things at the same time. The average person works seven jobs in their career and often there are industry switches, promotions, location changes, and technological changes that contribute to a changing landscape.

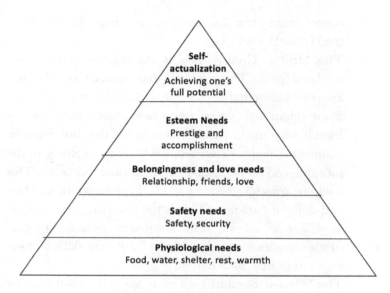

Maslow's Hierarchy of Needs

To provide some sort of a framework to decide what to do when you can't figure out which option to choose, we recommend taking a look at Maslow's Hierarchy of Needs. Coined by the psychologist Abraham Maslow in the 1940s, the hierarchy covers five key categories on an intrinsic level focusing on the individual intently. The categories range from basic, psychological, to self-fulfilment needs.

Think about the top portion of the pyramid that includes esteem needs and self-actualization. While these two sections are commonly lacking from a traditional job that helps most make ends meet, corporations have a way of limiting one's full talents and potential from ever being used. Oftentimes in large companies, there are so many people that their achievements are downplayed, or the direction of a genuine idea that could bring exponentially great results gets rejected because it does not meet the manager's criteria and is too far-fetched to try.

Think about how much money you need for your individual living expenses and how this will coincide with you running your business. For example, if it takes USD 40,000 to cover rent, food, and miscellaneous living expenses, you will need to find a way, either from temporary savings, working a regular job, relying on a spouse's income, leveraging existing capital from fundraising to keep you afloat while the revenue scales into a repeatable process so you can be self-sufficient off your business. If you fail to do this, then your startup will have an expiration date. In an interview with the founder of Infinitary Fund, a quantitative hedge fund just starting out, Michael Mills details working part-time at Starbucks to provide a stable income and healthcare for his family.

Sacrifices do need to be made but the idea is to one day create enough sustainable revenue and income for your business so that it can be sustainable long term.

In the end, make the decision that's best for you and take a look at the Maslow Hierarchy of Needs. If you find outsized gains in that decision towards a path to the top of the pyramid, self-actualization, then please go for it. If you're early in your career, it's worth getting a taste of the corporate life to understand how they operate and potentially take those systems and processes into your own corporation one day.

Food for thought: Where are you along the pyramid? What are the current risks? What are the rewards?

If, after reflection, you find yourself still interested in the world of startup, here's a taste of what life is like within the startup ecosystem.

There Are No Prerequisites for Being an Entrepreneur

The best part about being an entrepreneur is you're in charge. The worst part about being an entrepreneur is you're in charge. Contrary to popular belief that you have to go to college and get a degree, there is no direct path to having a successful company. All big companies were once small ideas born out of desperation or innate desire to provide the world with a solution to a problem. In fact, starting a company is easier than it's ever been today with the operating costs going down significantly. Outside of salaries and things like rent, initial costs would be low outside of product development and the cost of goods sold, which tend to include server storage. The lower the cash burn rate and the longer cash can stay in the bank means stability in the short term for the company.

Creativity Has No Boundaries

Innovation is contingent on the ability to find out if what's invented will work in the future. What's worked in the past has little or no bearing on what might work in the future. In a conversation with Jeremy Utley, Director of Executive Education at Stanford's Design School, in order to determine whether an idea is good or not, come up with ten ideas and try them all out. Run small experiments with different users and see what yields the best results. For example, to learn which copy for an email marketing campaign works best, send one email with a more salesy title and another with a more how-to approach.

Jobs Provide Stability, Startups Embrace Uncertainty

The traditional nine to five is the backbone of the global economy and a standard for work in the United States. Without it, there would be a severe lack of structure and probably some chaos. In the long run, jobs provide the regular person with a schedule and steady earnings—two things which are absolutely necessary to sustain a healthy lifestyle. Jobs provide the economy with growth and the nation as a whole is able to flourish from the interchange of capital.

However, the pandemic has given us a glimpse into a world that's been restructured. As commutes to an office became non-existent for most when lockdowns became the new normal, stability came in the form of working from home permanently. Google and Facebook ruled out the possibility of workers returning to the office indefinitely.

Thinking for Yourself and Working on Something You Love

We all have passions and interests that can be turned into stable income opportunities outside of working a day job.

The most commonly cited aspects of work that people hate include working with difficult people, feeling no impact from the results you've achieved, and a lack of belonging. Although these are things that can all be fixed to some extent, there is nothing like doing what you love every day and getting paid to do it. Corporate perks too wear off after a while. Studies have shown that if you are happier at home you tend to do better work. This is why it is important to build company culture at the beginning where co-founders and early employees enjoy what it is they are doing and who they are doing it with.

Ultimately, having the option to operate on your terms without pressure from a nagging boss is a double-edged sword.

A common subject among millennials, especially in a workforce generation that champions work from home and flexibility, are feelings of being stuck at a dead-end job coupled with doubts of ever breaking out of it with a job market that is noticeably tough on hiring. Is anyone ever going to let me do my dream job? What if I told you that you could create your own job as an entrepreneur? Would you hire yourself to do it?

It is common for the workforce to hold at least seven jobs in their lifetime. Moreover, workplace retention is at an all-time low with employees generally holding positions at the company for two years until finding a new job. This depicts the ever-changing employment landscape.

Good entrepreneurs don't want to be done, they want to do. Entrepreneurship is best perceived as a verb not a noun in the sense that it's the desire to work, not the end goal.

Because there is not one solution to the problem, entrepreneurship continues from the top and into the doer's hands.

You Do Not Always Need a Specific Background or Skill Set

Christina Lopes, the CEO and founder of the One Health Company, a startup in the biotech space attempting to cure canine cancer, would strike anyone she met as ambitious and charismatic about finding a cure for canine cancer.[14] But taking a step back, in a podcast we did with her, Christina remembers being in her twenties working as a barista at Starbucks having thoughts that this might be her life. Graduating from the University of Massachusetts, Boston, with an English degree, she eventually went on to work at Lehman Brothers and Credit Suisse on Wall Street.

But she credits her non-traditional background for giving her the ability to dream and do unconventional things.

She derives her grit from her parents and leaving a turbulent economy in Brazil in the 80s at an early age and moving to Boston, Massachusetts.

---

[14] Alex Knapp, 'Meet The Married Couple Who Just Raised $10 Million To Improve Cancer Treatments For Dogs', *Forbes*, 20 October 2020, https://www.forbes.com/sites/alexknapp/2020/10/29/meet-the-married-couple-who-just-raised-10-million-to-improve-cancer-treatments-for-dogs/?sh=56994dc84abb.

No one has all the skills, degrees, and BS accolades that are deemed worthy of starting a company. You start with what you're passionate about, what problems you'd like to see diminished; at the end of the day, all companies solve pain points with the aim to do so at scale. It may sound far-fetched to say, but everyone has passions and ideas on how to enhance either existing businesses or society. We are not advocating that everyone reading this become entrepreneurs but rather explore their curiosity in the real world and if not possessing all the skills like coding, that they either learn or find people equally as excited about the work.

Ben Lewis, who happens to be a co-founder and Christina's husband, noticed that on the one hand the One Health Company combines advances in genomics with those in AI to provide more personalized cancer treatments for dogs in conjunction with veterinarians and pharmacies, using insights gained from treating cancer in humans. The upshot is that as they do so, the data they gather can also be turned to the other end of the leash, providing insight in the treatment of human cancers as well.

In 2021, One Health Company received 8,500 phone calls from dog owners seeking help for their dogs with cancer.

Once they successfully raised a series A from Y Combinator and Andreessen Horowitz they continued to research therapies for canine cancer. One Health worked to sequence each cancer's genome and results found an actionable target that might respond to an existing drug. For example, for one dog, a treatment was applied, and two years later, it is alive, healthy, and barking for his dinner. They want to turn dogs from test subjects into patients. Since dogs are often test cases for medication prior to being applied in human use cases.

Startups ask for a different skill set from their people than traditional businesses. They embrace creative, disruptive individuals who are passionate about solving problems with technology.

What the World Is Trying to Tell You

Dan remembers the time when he used to live with his landlord who was extremely religious. She would spend the whole day in the upstairs kitchen. He recalls avoiding going to the kitchen if she was in there and even days and nights of waiting until she went downstairs to avoid seeing and talking to her.

The point being, when he and his family moved out, he felt instantly free from holding himself back. The truth is: perfect circumstances do not exist. Perfection does not exist either. What matters is the decision to improve your situation, whether it's moving out or continuously trying in the face of adversity.

These efforts build habits and cultivate your mindset to be geared for achievement. When Dan was uncomfortable wanting to avoid social situations and conversations, he desperately wanted to have control over his life. He could not land a job offer from a tech company no matter how hard he tried. He had to get out of that house to be in a place where he could have a clear mind and control what influenced him. If he could have gone back, he probably would have gotten a job as a waiter at a restaurant. There is no shame in working a normal blue-collar job that will help you stay afloat and financially well off. Society tends to frown upon work that is not some high paying job that allows a lot of freedom. This is completely wrong; to achieve success at any level one must work hard. In fact, being able to make the decisions and have the conversations is the success, the work is the success. Consistently doing things relating to your dreams every chance there is, is success. Yes, we need money to sustain our lives but truly doing work you believe in is the essence of what we recommend someone figure out first when starting a startup or new business venture.

What's funny is Dan landed a job in Hollywood. That's right! He met a celebrity at Los Angeles County Museum of Art and

Map Out Your Career Portfolio 53

convinced her to let him be her executive assistant on the spot. In an elevator at the LACMA, he said 'hi' to a woman and exchanged pleasantries, they talked about the museum and how the elevator was a work of art itself—the glass-enclosed elevator is surrounded by a three-storey red, black, and white art installation that changes as the elevator ascends or descends.

He had this feeling that he should talk to her more but went to a separate exhibit in the museum while she went in a different direction. Out of coincidence, he ran into her again at another exhibit.

He ended up mentioning he runs a podcast and the light bulbs lit up. He had said, he was just waiting for an opportunity, and she mentioned that she was looking for an assistant. They met three days later and he landed the job as an executive assistant to Kaila Methven.

It's these unexpected moments in life where we are caught off guard but can turn serendipity into an opportunity. The only way to know if your idea or proposal holds the value you imagine is to be **bold** and dare to present yourself in a way that is compelling. While it may be frightening to do something completely new and potentially life-changing in the moment; life will continue to present these moments and incorporating a bold mindset where you do everything you can to get what you want will lead to success.

Defining Your Focus Filter

Are you someone who has a portfolio of interests and projects that you want to work on? Do you think, *Life is too short anyway to limit myself to one project, right?* Chances are, if you're reading this book, you're ambitious in your professional—and personal—life. The question someone like you has to face is, how do I accomplish everything I want to accomplish? Earl, too, faces this challenge.

After a conversation with Earl's wife, she challenged him that perhaps it was time to focus not on the volume of projects but on the quality or types of projects that he will be spending his time on for the year. She encouraged him late last year to speak to one of our good friends and newly minted executive transformation coach, Kelly Lei.

Kelly encouraged him to do an exercise to prioritize not projects but really what mattered to him professionally, or in the end what impact did he want to have in his professional endeavours. He wrote down a few areas in general—like 'impact' or 'technology enabled' or 'digital transformation'—but in the end, it didn't seem to be right. After a couple weeks of questioning and reflection, he realized that you need to filter out projects so that you can narrow down what you should focus on, be it your main hustle or your side hustles. There are three distinct areas that you should be focusing on to find your filter, which he calls the **Focus Filter**.

- **Impact Scale:** How large of an impact do you want your initiatives to create in your lifetime? This is important so that you can filter the types of expectations you have for yourself and can trade off perhaps longer term projects and shorter term projects as well. This will also set the focus and expectation on the amount of tools, technology, and investment in time you might want to have to achieve a certain scale.
- **Community:** This is something that most people sometimes overlook but most people really have a strong feeling or bias towards. Have you asked yourself, what type of community do you want to impact? Is it to help out your local community or your town, is it your country, is it an industry? There is no wrong answer here, and you really would know deep inside what really is important.

- **Function:** How will you contribute to achieve your impact? What type of function are you planning to do to support your mission? Perhaps your strengths are already predisposed and you can grow to be the best in the world in that function to support the mission that you are hoping to achieve.

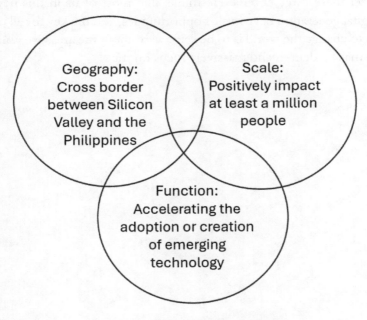

Example of Earl's Focus Filter

After weeks of reflection, Earl came up with his Focus Filter.

- **Impact Scale:** Will it positively impact at least a million people long-term?
- **Community:** Does the project impact my home country, the Philippines, directly or indirectly and does it relate to my current network in Silicon Valley?

- **Function:** Does it take advantage of my passion and skill in early-stage product development and the utilization of emerging technologies?

With this, it is easy to determine which projects Earl should work on. He promised himself that he will only work on projects that meet these three criteria. He thinks that most of us in this new digital generation have lots of opportunities, and the key for all of us to change the world is to be self-aware about the areas we want to make a dent in and massively focus on this.

7

Action Trumps Talk.
Don't Be a Wannapreneur.

'I was a serious comic collector and fanboy as a kid. I wanted very badly to draw comic books for a lot of my childhood and early adolescence. So when you have an unfulfilled dream like that, years later you find yourself in a position to make a graphic novel—hell yeah, I'm going to do that.'
—Anthony Bourdain

We have all seen this. Friends or family that keep on talking about ideas for years but never do anything about it, but when they see that their idea gets implemented by another person, they keep on claiming that they had that idea for decades and if only life was different, they would have been a billionaire like Elon Musk or Jeff Bezos.

We call them Wannapreneurs, people who want to be entrepreneurs, they want to take the risk, but always have a reason not to continue and make it happen. While we know that life circumstances are different for many people, it is important to be honest with oneself if we are in love with being an entrepreneur or if we actually want to do the hard work to actually become one.

It's not a real company until you incorporate and have customers.

An important lesson Dan has learned on his journey as an entrepreneur is that you can have ideas, services, and products but not having a holding structure set up by filing an LLC will not give you a company. Although it may seem like common sense to most, and a risky decision to some, starting a company is simply filing the paperwork to do so.

Starting a company is not necessarily getting office space or leasing a storefront or even starting a website. The first step to finding your niche is cementing the idea into reality by creating a corporation. Don't worry, it's simple and can be done in about five business days. We recommend using Swyft as it is what Startup Mindsets LLC was incorporated with.

Immediately after we filed the paperwork and were approved, Dan felt a rush incomparable to anything else he had done before. It was breaking away from being employed by someone else and taking his money-making future into his own hands, which was empowering. He recalls waking up the first few days being eager to get this thing off the ground. We recommend if you have an idea that keeps you up at night or a problem that you want to tackle at scale, start by forming an LLC or Delaware C Corp (best for startups). This is all starting a company is and it is not that difficult or worth contemplating a long time over. It doesn't hurt to put money into an idea that can set you up for the long run. It sets you up for the long run and gives you access to write offs and business tools like Stripe, which require you to have an EIN or Tax ID number to use to process your first payments if you are going to build software and accept payments online. Additionally, it is important to separate yourself from the business for it to function as an entity away from you for tax and legal purposes.

Are you ready to be CEO?

Growing up, we all have this perception that a chief executive officer happens to be a rich person who orders people around and takes credit for a company's success. It's not uncommon because movies and general assumptions would indicate that having the highest title within an organization yields power and influence. Being a startup founder means that to get the idea off the ground, you have got to do everything. This can mean being an engineer at night and a sales person by day, aka a jack of all trades. Chief executives in big corporations don't have their work scattered across different business functions as much but do manage the company as a whole. Being a CEO is being a leader.

In November 2016, Earl was back in the Manila startup scene since he had left almost a year prior. As he then reflected on certain highs and lows during the time he was founder and president of IdeaSpace, which has now grown to be the top startup acceleration programme in the Philippines, he realized that building a company out of nothing but an idea and a PowerPoint, seeing how the company grew, is such a great experience. He realized, though, that if he had to do things all over again, he would redo some of my actual moves. Here are his reflections:

1. Being called 'chief' something needs to be earned. When Earl was twenty-nine, he was placed as Head of Innovation for SMART, a telecom company with 70 million subscribers and he was one of the youngest, if not the youngest, VP-level executives in the Philippines. Being naive and crazy, he asked his boss in a one-on-one, his initials were 'MVP', if he could also be called the Chief Innovation Officer of the group or at least CEO of IdeaSpace. His boss smiled for a bit, and told him, 'Earl, a C-level title is earned not just given out lightly.'

He was a bit shocked at that time. He was thinking, *all my startup friends had chief this, chief that, even cool names like 'Chief Hacker'*. After years though, he realized that his boss was right, it gave him more motivation as 'president' to earn his stripes, to not settle, to make bold moves, and to show results, and maybe then, he'd earn his C-level status.

2. Being on the top is extremely lonely. Find your peer advisers. During his time as President of IdeaSpace, there were times when he didn't know whom he should talk to for advice—especially for large personal or professional decisions. He was lucky that his wife at home, every night, always asked how he was and how she could help. Professionally, he struggled with some decisions, especially tough ones. He'd think sometimes, *it's too small a decision to raise to my board but too big a decision that my team might misinterpret my thoughts as an actual decision.* He was lucky that during these times, he had his peer advisers, a group of people he trusted and could share his pains and stories with. He had dinners with some of the founding teams—Paul, who ran the developer network at SMART; Nick, who was head of PR; and Marthyn, who was co-founder and a CIO of the electric utility and second youngest executive in the group. He also found solace in peer networks, where at that critical time, he was nominated for the World Economic Forum Young Global Leader Program, and he then discovered that all over the world, founders and presidents had similar struggles and he always had great advice from his friends in this network.

3. Go back to first principles—your mission and your key values—and make decisions based on them. When he started IdeaSpace, they did a number of press releases, a number of interviews, and a number of presentations. It was actually funny. But all the time, the press asked, 'Why

does IdeaSpace exist?' And with a clear conviction, in front of the TV cameras and journalists, we said the same message over and over again—'To build a new Philippines economy based on science and technology, to change the culture so that engineers, scientists, and technologists will be an inspiration to the next generation and [have] the same status as artists, models, and basketball players.' Our values were 'Global ambition, speed of execution, and frugality.' These were the first principles, the foundation of the company, that guided his decision as president all the time. He sees that very few founders spend time on this, in the tough times, this guided his decision.

4. Develop 'Founder Amnesia'. Constantly refine your story. Having pitched over 200 venture capitalists and received hundreds of noes to funding, it's important to refresh your mindset and not let the past affect your head.

5. Be prepared to make the tough calls that even your team might disagree with but you know are right even while others think you are crazy. CEOs and founders have the struggle of making tough decisions all the time, but one trait that he sees in his other founder friends is a strong conviction of the future state that you want to help build. One such decision was to support a call from our government—from his friend Mike Ignacio, the former trade attaché to Silicon Valley—to help with a conference called 'SlingshotMNL', which was envisioned to be the Startup and Innovation Showcase for the Asia-Pacific Economic Cooperation (APEC) Summit, which so happens to be hosted in the Philippines. The task by the APEC team was, 'We need your help, we have two months to pull off this world-class conference but we need a private-sector partner.'

He thought that everyone would say yes, but for a variety of reasons, no one but he committed time and resources for this. So, even his team in a staff meeting said, 'Why are we doing this, how will this benefit IdeaSpace?' He didn't know what to say but he just said, 'I don't know if there is really a benefit to us as IdeaSpace and there may be zero but I know that this would benefit the Philippines.' He knew in his gut it was the right call, mission-driven and important, but he had a 2 per cent doubt about why the other companies didn't join and devote resources, but he did and could see that maybe this was a way to show that the startup industry is real. After two months, and a *lot* of help from his friends and professors from Stanford—especially Nicolás Shea, the founder of Start-Up Chile, Prof. Richard Dasher from Stanford, and friends in Southeast Asia—2,000 people applied for a 1,000-person capacity conference that was the springboard to what now is QBO, the National Innovation Centre of the Philippines.

6. Place rejection in context. Use your judgment as to why that 'no' happened. Once you break down most of those reasons, it's hard to take them personally. Take the time to take the emotion out of it and assess why it is happening.

7. Have intellectual humility to know what you don't know. Being CEO doesn't mean you know all the answers. It's okay to admit when you need help or don't know the topic. As CEO, your job is not to *have* the answers but to *look* for the answers. Earl came to this realization a few months into the job. He thought that having co-run the Cisco I-Prize, the Global Innovation competition of Cisco in hundred countries, he *knew* how to run a National Call for Innovation startups. He placed his 'online form' and had a massive launch, and after two months and tons of Facebook boosts and ads, less than hundred applications

Action Trumps Talk. Don't Be a Wannapreneur.

came in. He was distraught and ready to write off this experiment called 'IdeaSpace' and ready to go back to focusing full time on his telecom job. He asked his board for advice, and they said, 'Earl, you must do national roadshow first?' Earl said in his mind, *Roadshow? That's so pre-internet.* With hesitation, he said okay, but was sceptical about the potential result.

One of the first roadshows was in a public university in Davao, the University of Southeastern Philippines, one of the top five schools in the country, but over 90 per cent of the students were on scholarships due to affordability. One student asked him in the open panel, 'I am hopeful with your vision of IdeaSpace and glad you're willing to invest in my idea, but what if I cannot pay you back, I don't have money, my family has no money?' He smiled and responded, 'You don't need to pay it back because I am investing in you and your idea through equity, which means that if it goes to zero we make zero, but if it goes well, we both do well.' He was teary-eyed, shocked, and lit up by this college sophomore, and she said, 'This is a dream come true for us.' This was the moment, he knew what he had been planning for was for something bigger than the first year after his countless roadshows and time away from family would be worth it. That first year, the programme got close to 700 applicants for IdeaSpace and was a valuable lesson on how important intellectual humility is for a CEO. At this point, Earl realized that the board was correct. While we have certain biases towards how we did things in the past, one must be constantly open to ideas, and let the data and results lead decision-making.

8. Know the point at which you should leave, and that decision should still be about the original mission you set

out to accomplish. One of the scariest decisions of his life was when he was contemplating leaving IdeaSpace to pursue an opportunity to work and learn from one of the largest funds in the world in New York. He was thinking, *Four years I have spent building this, I can't leave now.* When he got the offer and was struggling with his decision, his wife looked him in the eye and asked, 'Are you thinking of staying in the country because of your rock star status or because you think that staying here is good for the Philippines?' She continued to say, 'Are you here because of ego or because of mission?' She knew that for him to be better for the Philippines, he had to re-learn, to experience a new beginning, to be a student now and not a teacher any more, to grow again—and to stay true to the mission, to be better for the country, so that one day, he'd come back again and be a better person.

After a couple of weeks, Earl had an appointment with his boss and chairman of IdeaSpace 'MVP', and he imagined in his mind that since his boss hired him from the US, he'd ask him to also stay. He had his points laid out but was hoping deep inside he'd make a big fuss out of this. Earl opened the door and he asked him, 'Are you thinking of leaving us?' He was prepared for his logical debate, but before he knew it, he asked him another question. 'How old are you, Earl?' He said he was thirty-three. His boss said, 'Go to New York, learn some more, you are young, and when you are ready, bring back these experiences and do good things, we'll be here when you are ready to come back.' Just like that, Earl gave him his resignation letter and left. He was no longer the president of the company that he grew from a PowerPoint that he and his co-founder, Marthyn, had pitched for USD 12 million in funding, thirty-eight teams, over 2,500 applications, and hundreds of events and hundreds of thousands of innovators he met throughout their national roadshows—all in the span of three and a half years. But, it was time to grow and re-learn, not for himself but for the mission, the country.

In 2016, Geeks on a Beach Part 4 was being organized. Our original idea had come out of a funny conversation between five people on how cool it was to have people hang out on the beach and talk tech. After four years, over 500 people were flying to Bohol to attend this, and Earl was lucky that he was joining it with added reflections and was in the process of becoming a better version of himself to hopefully plan it out one day. He was back again, permanently, to these shores to continue the mission of 'building a new economy based on science, innovation, and technology'.

Are You Choosing Excellence?

In the past eight years, Earl has coached, mentored, invested in, and advised dozens of startup companies in a number of countries. Most of them are early-stage and run by the original founders. There is something he calls the 'survivor mentality', which goes like this: 'As long as I can survive until the next milestone, then we're good.' Or it goes something like this: 'Let's focus on this small thing, and IF and ONLY when that is reached, then we can think big.'

One difference that he noticed, though, in some of the startups that end up doing well is the mindset of the founders—particularly the CEO and/or CTO, as they strive for excellence or to be the 'best in the world'—towards building the business. A startup, or even a company in general, is *hard* and for sure the odds are not in their favour, so the question Earl always asks the startups before he agrees to be their adviser is 'Where do you think this startup will be going five years from now?' What he looks for is not necessarily what they say, but the conviction

66 Startup Mindsets

he sees in the eyes of the founder that they truly will achieve their global ambitions with their startups.

He shares below what it might feel like to interact with a CEO who is wired for survival mode:

1. Talking about why you 'can't' do things all the time versus thinking of creative ways to make them work.
2. Obsessed about the next funding round versus focused on customer satisfaction or building product.
3. Thinking of random projects because of the revenue implications versus building a strategic roadmap of products that all fit in the end.
4. At some point, operations take over and strategy goes out of the door. He's not saying that doing these activities is bad, but he's saying to be conscious as a founding team if these behaviours become the majority of the conversations.

For the 'excellence' mindset founders, he's seen some of these behaviours that he would like to note as potential best practices.

1. Knowing the strengths and weaknesses of a team and complementing the weaknesses through training, getting advisers or board of directors, or strategic hiring. He's seen that some of the first hires make a higher base salary than the founding team themselves.
2. Being thought-leading in the market globally. The founding team, not just the CEO or Head of Sales, should test the idea every week or month and validate with the open market all the time and sell the vision. The way to do this is to aim to be the experts in the market and technical domains.
3. Have a clear vision and product roadmap and milestones that you are building against over time, and this dictates

the funding strategy. This also combats our natural tendency to figure things out quickly.
4. Unite every member of the team towards the same goals and call them to action. Every member in the initial team must know why they are there and what their role in the organization is.

The challenge for future and current founders is to always ask themselves, 'Am I operating in a "survival mindset" or am I operating in the "excellence mindset"? Hopefully, this frame of reference can help you and your team focus on what's most important to your company and why you exist in the first place.

Are You Embracing Scrappiness?

There are stories about the startups that started in a garage, such as Google and Apple. What makes a garage a great place is that it promotes urgency and relentlessness that are hard to invoke in a fancy office with perks. Not to say there isn't hustle or scrappiness in an office but when things are just starting from the idea phase and no well-outlined business plan is present, the spirit of entrepreneurship is tangible and pushes founders to get to the next checkpoint.

When we interviewed James Wang, a venture capitalist at Creative Ventures who had spent time as an employee at Google X's Makani project, Google's Moonshot factory, about working as an entrepreneur compared to working in a large corporation, James alluded to the fact that large corporations can essentially prolong innovation projects because most likely the revenue won't affect their top or bottom line noticeably enough unless it becomes a multibillion dollar business segment. Moreover, if you take away the urgency, it's less important to figure out who your right market is and how do you turn this into a business that can make money now. You can forever put off the most important priorities if you're operating with a mindset of 'I can refine this technology more, network, and the deadline holds less significance because there needs to be internal stakeholder alignment, etc.'

Income or the ability to raise funding derives from the ability to make sales and take that money into your personal bank account, which directly correlates to your lifestyle. What likely guides an entrepreneur to market a new technology is the need for cash now to further sustain the company and those who are working to operate it. If it does not work out, then cash will eventually dry up causing lots of stress on the founders and even investors.

Do You Have a Personal Board of Advisers?

Advisers can range from industry leaders who have expertise on a certain subject matter. This tends to include university professors who have researched and experienced the science part of the company.

For instance, at Flux Technology we had professors from MIT and UC Berkeley advise on product development. Having a board demonstrates to potential investors that there are other industry experts with high credentials like PhDs that exist to provide guidance on core technologies and innovations that are not common knowledge.

Not all boards are limited to industry expertise but boards can really act as support systems. As different aspects of the business unfold, your mindset will shift, as it is human nature. The benefit of having a set of advisers is the advice they can provide in making important decisions. There can be a different set of advisers for the go-to market and navigating the industry.

The Most Critical Questions to Ask a Co-Founder

One of the most common reasons why a company fails is not because of the quality of the technology or the size of the market but because of a misalignment between the co-founders of the company.

In October 2019, Earl had to deal with two strong startup teams that were dealing with a 'co-founder break-up' without having to ruin the company.

Let's face it, every person has a different reason for why they start or join the founding team of a company. Some want to 'change the world'. Some want 'to build things that impact millions of lives'. To be honest, many people are in it to have the chance to win the venture lotto, hitting the jackpot of having more than 1 per cent of shares when a company gets listed or acquired, acquiring 'life-changing wealth'.

Of course, 99 per cent of startups fail, so it might have been better for most to just work a corporate job. Regardless, it's very important to know what each other's motivations are before you commit and spend ten to twelve (or more) hours per day with a group of people for at least three to five years.

When Earl was starting Plentina, a new fintech startup focused on alternative credit scoring and micro-lending in the Philippines, I met one of my Stanford friends who had successfully built a company and exited her startup. She gave me very important advice on co-founder alignment.

She also exclaimed that it is important to develop this transparency early on because, like marriage, there is typically a 'honeymoon period' of twelve to eighteen months where everything seems to be fine. But when sh#t hits the fan, then this conversation becomes most important to come back to and understand each other.

Here are the most important questions to ask while having a sit-down with your co-founder when you start or shortly thereafter. Earl's advice is to do a 'double-blind test' where each one of you writes down the answers separately and then discuss it.

- How does this startup align with your personal purpose?
- Why are you personally building this startup?

- What is a good outcome for the startup and when do you expect this to happen?
- What is your end goal in ten years and how does this startup help you achieve it?
- Any life changes over the course of the startup that we must anticipate?
- What are the non-negotiables for you (meaning the situations or values where you will stop everything)?
- What are the areas you are best at and areas you are weak at?
- How can I as your co-founder help you achieve your ten-year goal?

Starting a company is hard and often comes with many risks. It is undoubtedly an emotional roller coaster. I hope that you all get to ask these questions to each other early on; not just to avoid heartache later on but also be able to focus on building the business rather than dealing with co-founder drama.

8

The Power of Place

'Everyone is a genius. But if you judge a fish by its ability to climb a tree, it will live its whole life believing it is stupid.'

—Albert Einstein

Thousands of entrepreneurs flock to San Francisco and Silicon Valley from all over the world with hopes they can raise venture capital and attract top talent in the form of engineers, product designers, and other experts. They physically leave their current cities, automatically placing themselves out of their comfort zone. Taking a step like this is a 'shit just got real' moment. In the Bay Area, ideas and capital are exchanged like no other place in the world. The venture firms on Sand Hill Road, like Sequoia and Andreessen Horowitz, are constantly searching for the next Ubers or Airbnbs while thousands of startups are looking for a lifeline and long-term partnership. Pre-pandemic, thousands of people wanting a job at these hot startups and tech companies were fleeing their homes to fill positions in these fields alone. While remote and distributed work have restructured the pitch and network in-person work style to online, the best way to build rapport is still being in places that allow for serendipity.

Prior to the pandemic, this was the case; having the ability to do in-person pitches with investors or customers mattered.

Moreover, meeting peers in the space and networking in a room full of potential customers, friends, and supporters meant you were doing something right. But because Covid-19 halted in-person gatherings, venture firms instantly shifted to virtual meetings and the notion of needing to meet in person was removed from our consciousness.

Then came the question: Do you need to be in Silicon Valley to benefit from all the resources that come with its proximity? Jason Calacanis, one of the most renowned angel investors, is famous for saying in an excerpt of his blog, 'Raising money is still much easier when your HQ is based in the Valley.' But during Covid-19, VCs wouldn't even take an in-person pitch.

The value of being in the Bay Area as an entrepreneur is less valid nowadays, since meetings and in-person work traditionally conducted in an office or coffee shop, are now held virtually. However, as there is a high concentration of tech talent in Silicon Valley and history of technological innovation, it does not hurt to be here either. It pays dividends to be among peers who are aiming for the same goals as startup entrepreneurs because proximity and like-minded individuals have the ability to motivate and remind you that your work matters.

When Earl was seventeen, he went on a vacation to California to see his brother, who at that time was interning for the Stanford Basketball team. Little did Earl know that the trip would change his life in more ways than one. On a tour of the campus, he entered the engineering quad and saw the two buildings that welcome visitors on each side—one building has the name Hewlett and the other Packard. He asked his brother, 'Is this where HP was born?' He said, 'Yes, long ago they were students at this university, built one of the iconic tech companies in a garage close to campus in Palo Alto, California, and from that environment, the company Hewlett Packard was born.'

That day at Stanford, he had a feeling inside that he could not explain. It seemed that it wasn't the air or the sunshine that was different, but it was a place where he felt his creative energy could be channelled the right way, and he could be surrounded by people, corporations, and professors who foster this type of environment for ideas to thrive.

Another way to explain this is to look at this as an ecosystem—a collection of different ingredients that get together over time and are interdependent on each other for the ecosystem to grow and flourish, like the different species of animals and plants inside a rainforest, where each one of them is interrelated to the other. It's no wonder, a study[15] shows Stanford alumni creating nearly USD 3 trillion in economic impact each year. A study by two Stanford professors determines that companies founded by the university's alumni generate trillions in annual revenue and have created 5.4 million jobs.

Later that day, he trekked a few miles and saw the famous HP Garage, which is called the birthplace of Silicon Valley. He wondered how such a massive corporation back then could be the start of the whole tech industry in the San Francisco Bay Area. The garage is now more of a symbol to many would-be startup entrepreneurs that ideas can be built from simple beginnings with a small number of people in an unfancy place like a garage or a kitchen table or inside a dormitory of a school. No need to rent a penthouse floor in a building in midtown New York City to be your starting point to change the world. Of course, many of the top companies such as Apple, Google, Facebook started in a garage or makeshift offices, they all started with this first step to build something in a place and now are household names in most of our everyday digital lives.

These almost myth-like stories of success are the basis of a culture that amplifies a set of norms, customs, and incentive

---

[15] Jamie Beckett, 'Study Reports Stanford Alumni Create Nearly $3 trillion in Economic Impact', Standford Engineering, 22 October 2012, https://engineering. stanford.edu/magazine/study-reports-stanford-alumni-create-nearly-3-trillion-economic-impact.

74 Startup Mindsets

structures in this environment. However, remember that anyone with a dream and know-how can potentially be the next Google founder, and this idea creates more of an idealistic and somewhat close to a meritocratic culture that feeds on the basis of Silicon Valley. Finding the environment that allows you to be yourself unapologetically unlocks the mindset you need to perform at a high level on a consistent basis.

Sometimes all you have to do to change your mindset is to go somewhere new for a while. We tend to get caught up with who we are and believe that we are only capable of achieving so much when we have been in a place for too long. Getting out of our comfort zones and breaking traditional thought habits by simply being somewhere else allows for new strategies and ideas. It allows for more focus to be exerted, along with deeper curiosity and a greater chance of being able to try something new.

Place Is Really Community

Blue Zones are areas in the world with the highest concentration of centenarians, or people who live to more than hundred years old. Before the pandemic hit, Earl was lucky to visit one of these blue zones in Sardinia, an island of Italy. Many thought that the secret to getting to an old age is to not eat any meat, only eat vegetables, and have no alcohol. What he observed when he was there was that the food was amazing, consisting of delectable Italian (or Sardinian) delicacies, which consist of carbs; and some studies even show that the people there drink wine regularly.

As someone who spends most of their time trying to figure out how to 'hack the body' in order to become healthier, this puzzled Earl, because most of the mainstream media focuses on the way of scarcity like dieting or rapid exercising mostly in gyms. These activities are of course better than doing nothing, but what Earl found out is that one of the key secrets of these amazing blue zones comes from a few factors that are related to a startup mindset.

The Power of Place 75

Compared to some cultures, Earl really felt that some of these areas have a strong sense of community, a sense of purpose of what contribution each one of them has to the greater and immediate society. Maybe it's a baker who wakes up at 4 a.m. to prepare the bread and the town knows to go to him to get the freshest bread. This might not be a 'saving the world' purpose, but it gives each person reasons to keep on going no matter what age they are. Also, the sense of community happens when a sense of watching out for each other is there. Imagine a place where because everyone is engrained in the fabric of each of their daily lives, neighbours can check up on each other to make sure that they are okay.

Today's American society lacks that sense of community not necessarily because we are socially distant or have our noses in our phones but because communities like these are made hard to exist in America. Being able to afford a place to stay means an hour-long commute, so people hardly spend time in their neighbourhoods. What small teams like startups have by default is the sense of having each other's backs because you may have no choice but to grab lunch with your co-worker. Build an environment that makes your team want to make meaningful contributions. Business people need other people they can engage in conducive brainstorming with. Ultimately, building a team that cares for each other beyond work is how everyone starts to enjoy each other's company and an environment begins to mean something more than just a place.

On a personal level, one of the most important determining factors in shaping your mindset is ensuring your environment encourages strong habits towards not only work ethic but striking the balance between being able to express yourself, knowing that your work matters, and having the support system to keep going on the most difficult days. This includes a positive support system or a community of individuals that support what it is you're doing.

76 Startup Mindsets

The biggest value of being based in the Bay Area is being able to witness a number of people who are able to start companies and be successful. Each of their unique impacts on society can be felt noticeably and subtly, and in turn inspire you.

9

Let Data and Market Feedback Be Your Guide

'How happy had it been for me had I been slain in the battle. It had been far more noble to have died the victim of the enemy than fall a sacrifice to the rage of my friends.'

—Alexander the Great

The five most valuable companies by market capitalization (shares outstanding x share price) in 2022 were Amazon, Apple, Microsoft, Google, and Meta. What these companies have done well is creating products around the user's tendencies thus tailoring an experience that promotes more product usage. As an early-stage startup, it is key to let the users dictate what components to implement and where to hold off.

The 2010s, a decade characterized by the rapid adoption of technology on a global scale, saw existing legacy businesses fighting to stay afloat. New lines of code comprise primarily digital products that can be adopted at mass scale with ease. But it is also the innovation that existing corporations produce and adopt that keeps consumers happy and profits on the rise. As large companies innovate from within, innovation and new products fight to compete. This sparks the question, 'Should someone be an entrepreneur on their own or try to build a new idea inside the company?' The answer depends on how ambitious the person is and the feedback they receive from inside the company, if they'll pay enough attention to the idea in the first place. Software developers are on the front lines of creating code that makes products work and therefore sell.

While some new entrepreneurs break away from these corporations to start their own startup / side business to discover their passion and attempt to solve challenges unique to them, there is always a constant debate about whether to remain comfortable working a stable, well-paying job or quit and hopefully find happiness in more noble pursuits. For example, Tingwei Huang, a director of AI / machine learning at Amazon Web Services, details Amazon's culture by saying, 'Anyone with an idea can literally come up with a business proposal and submit it to management.' This type of behaviour is actually encouraged, as Amazon is willing to pay employees to come up with new business segments. Perhaps one of the most important pieces of advice Tingwei offered on our podcast was that during her time at Amazon, they honed in on being obsessed with serving the customer. For a company that has billions of users, this sounds impossible. However, Amazon's team works around the clock to understand buyer behaviour and new ways to improve user experience.

It is important to test out ideas and welcome proper feedback on the product before attempting to go big. Most founders start by sharing a product with friends who can use the first iteration, and learn from their opinions to make product tweaks and this cycle continues.

Limit Blind Spots

It is important to surround yourself with people who help you see what you cannot and engage in meaningful discussions.

On the road, the cars with the biggest blind spots are ones with long backsides such as trucks and SUVs. While these vehicles may have the most power, they are hard to manoeuvre at times. In the startup world, being talented with technical skills won't take you to great heights without being able to listen to feedback, whether from customers, advisers, or your valuable teammates. However, be sure to filter what feedback is important and focus on the vision.

There are a lot of openings in the market to solve huge problems with technology. However, validating that a problem exists outside of one's personal opinion does not happen automatically for someone with a perceived solution. Prior to founding Line, now named Beem—a fintech startup that provides instant micro loans to workers with fluctuating income like an Uber driver, a Starbucks barista, etc.—Akshay Krishnaiah lived in the shoes of his future users by driving 36,000 miles as an Uber driver himself in the San Francisco Bay Area. This took a year or so after departing from a full-time job at PayPal. While driving passengers to their destination, he conducted his own research by asking riders if they would be interested in an instant access line of cash or credit to help pay the bills or buy needed goods. When riders responded with similar responses revolving around being strapped for cash and struggling to make ends meet, Akshay realized that workers with fluctuating income needed access to instant cash for short-term expenses such as rent, groceries, or transportation. Thus, Line was born.

During his breaks from driving Uber, Akshay would work at the Dunkin' Donuts in South San Francisco, building the product, business plan, and talking to investors over donuts and coffee. This process was not the glamorous lifestyle that came with a fancy tech building with lounge chairs and catered lunch as it used to be at his former job at PayPal. It involved the grit and grind of building nothing into something. Traction came from support by angel investors from Sequoia and Uber.

During the summer of 2020, Line was accepted into Techstars Western Union accelerator and secured USD 120,000 in funding in exchange for giving up 7 per cent equity. The accelerator, while conducting everything virtually, benefited Akshay greatly. Techstars provided mentorship with experts in fintech to bounce ideas off of and offer products, go-to market, and business advice on demand. But perhaps the greatest benefit of joining an accelerator was that it put a tribe behind him. A group of friends and mentors who had gone through similar journeys helped inspire him to face the daily rigour head on.

Being surrounded by other founders in the same space optimized him as an individual, not just helping the company gain traction or fundraising. Opportunities to learn from how other startups overcome their challenges allows room for inspiration and focus to be doubled. Without the endless offerings of mentorship readily available, navigating the startup journey would be more daunting and demanding.

In the nine months since launch in 2020, Line has amassed 56,000 users and is helping people make ends meet without going into a major financial hole. Users pay a USD 5.99 subscription fee and get up to USD 500 instant access line, no FICO or credit check. If you are interested, check them out at https://trybeem.com.

'It helped to get under the skin of the user for a long time.' This means understanding how users benefit from the product and this takes at least six months. To be a great business, minimize risk by trying to get 20/20 vision, which can only be achieved by working people who are likely to close their blind spots. They provide an iterative feedback loop, offering encouragement and positive sentiments on the business' growth prospects. Your job is to listen to them.

In an interview we did with Luke Diaz, an early employee at the startup Optimizely who eventually became head of customer success, he mentioned, 'If users don't experience proper onboarding, they are more likely to churn. About 40 per cent of churn can be traced back to failed onboarding. The onboarding process includes customers changing their habits. They're learning a brand new software experience, and you also have to coach them to share the impact of that software with their peers.'

If you don't get off the ground, there's a high likelihood of customers leaving after the contract expires. The trick with startups in the enterprise software space is to invest in improving user experience and outcomes by guiding them through tools instead of letting them just figure it out on their own. On the business-to-consumer side of things, it is still important to incentivize users to use your product, think Doordash and its discount codes for first timers or an SMS strategy that asks users for survey feedback.

All Feedback Is Good Until it Is Not

When the feedback is negative, the sales don't go your way, it is difficult to decide what to do based on that feedback. Emotions may get in the way of it, either seeking to prevent yourself from being let down or affecting one's confidence when presenting the idea. But the fact that you're open to receiving feedback means that there are pros and cons and in order to be a successful startup it may mean accepting the information and tweaking the strategy to deliver what's necessary.

In a podcast we did with Shaun Gold, a serial entrepreneur and now Head of Content at Open VC, Shaun shared how entrepreneurs have to be able to reflect and plunge. Entrepreneurs need to filter out and distil objectively, what's going wrong and what to do to be in growth mode. One must adjust accordingly to tweak the product, the pitch deck, and oneself while placing it into context of the next opportunity.

Understand what to do based on reflection and analysis, then execute.

10

Find Your Superpower and Kryptonite

'I was aware of my success, but I never stopped trying to get better.'
—Michael Jordan

Earl was chatting with one of the venture capitalists in New York, who asked him a strange question: 'Earl, what is your superpower? And what is your kryptonite?'

Honestly, Earl didn't know how to react at first, but after deep reflection, he realized the importance of this question, not just at that meeting but for life in general. It is important for each of us to keep a sense of self-honesty, a realization that we are mostly great at a few things, but we also have areas that we are just not built to be strong at naturally.

Finding Your Superpower

Amazing people who truly embrace startup mindsets are always on a path to discover this one thing called their own unique superpower. Earl was a big comic book fan since he was young, so he dreamt at that age that he would have a cool new superpower. Although it might be ridiculous to think of yourself as a superhero like Superman, Batman, or the Avengers, he thinks all of us have

84 Startup Mindsets

been given an extremely unique set of circumstances and areas that we can only call our own. Our one in a 7.8 billion stories.

When we think of a superhero, we always see what's specific and unique to them. For example, Thor can control his hammer and use it to generate lightning bolts or you can have someone like Superman who can fly, have X-ray vision, and be able to have super strength.

When Earl thinks of a superpower in the real world, he thinks you have to answer three unique questions and the intersection is your superpower:

1. **What activities do you find easy to do and like doing?** There are certain things in our lives that just come naturally to us. We might be exposed to a certain activity and realize that we naturally excel at it as a beginner and enjoy doing it. Once you discover your natural ability or abilities, you can then put in the 10,000 hours of practice that it takes to be an expert and dominate. Whatever the path is to uncover this, it is essential to be open to discover it yourself and create an understanding that both nature and nurture might be in place for you to get this power. Unique abilities might come the day you are born, but the key is to be able to then have the right amount of freedom to explore and practise them to galvanize your skill or power.

   Can you find something you can truly be world class in and at the same time carry a burning curiosity? This is where the intersection of skill and passion are vital to creating a product and other legs of the business. The desire to always be learning and executing on all levels are characteristics that serve founders and revolutionary organizations that change the world.

   Many of us only discover our superpowers in our twenties, and some even go through their entire lives not

Find Your Superpower and Kryptonite

knowing, but one thing's for certain, it's that the quest to find your own unique superpower is so important as a startup because it is important to leverage it and find the right balance in the team to make sure that all bases are covered.

When Dan started the *Startup Mindsets* podcast, he walked into it knowing that he liked talking to people. This was right before podcasting exploded into what it is today, with 740 million different podcasts unlike a time when it was just an experiment done virtually over Zoom.

He's found it easy to spark conversation with people but perhaps his superpower has been asking questions and listening to people. At first, he would get nervous to interview some people because he felt they were so much more accomplished than he was—they were venture capitalists or executives managing large sums of money and in positions of power in the business world. He'd often ramble when speaking to these perceived VIPs, so much so that a feedback to him from Prof. Euvin, a former faculty member at Harvard, was that he needed to be more concise when talking to people. Eventually, he found his stride being able to bring confidence into the conversations, having done so many episodes and receiving positive feedback from fans like, 'Man, I'm a huge fan of the show.' You know you're good at something when highly accomplished CEOs from startups start asking to be on the podcast and complimenting you.

He found podcasting comes naturally to him because he enjoys learning by hearing people share their stories. Now that he's honed in on that superpower, he has some incredible opportunities in the form of advertising partnerships and cross collaborations. Curiosity trumps fears and doubts because it is impossible to have those two when we don't assume the outcome of an email or

86 Startup Mindsets

event. Add curiosity to what stands in your way because it'll make you genuinely wonder and make it easier to try.

2. **What do your friends and colleagues say you are good at?**
Like a startup, the only way for you to really know that your hunches are correct is with external validation. This could come in the form of your friends telling you how excellent you are in a certain area or teachers cheering you on a specific subject or the best one could be if you are sought out by external parties to share your expertise about a certain topic. All of these scenarios lead to an area where the way to be sure that you might be on to your superpower is to also understand that others see it the same way as you.

During the pandemic, when both of us decided to launch the *Startup Mindsets* podcast, it was clear that many of their friends supported us. Many of the first guests were close friends or someone whom we'd spoken to before. When we mentioned we were going to host this startup and venture related audio programme that talks about the 'why' and mindsets of entrepreneurs, many got it right away that we were the right hosts for a topic like this. Why is that? Because many of our friends knew very quickly how passionate we both are in democratizing this information to the world, and that perhaps both of us have certain personalities that would make us good hosts. This probably is related to the consistent background that we both have had, where Dan is an English major turned investor but has lived his whole life in the Valley, and Earl, being an executive and entrepreneur, has been both a speaker but also a moderator or a speaker for many startup conferences in the past. There was no doubt that

Find Your Superpower and Kryptonite

none of our friends were surprised and were extremely supportive of this new-found venture of ours.

3. **What life experiences have you had that are unique to you and reinforce 1 and 2?**

As much as most of us might think otherwise, we have similar life experiences to others, all of us are collections of distinct and discrete experiences that, when added as a whole, are extremely unique only to us compared to any of the other 8 billion people existing today. We have to explore how we think if we are only a unit of one, what would be the combination that we can offer that no one else on Earth can replicate? How can we create an 'n=1' story, the collection of life choices and experiences that make it very different from anyone else in the world?

When Earl was invited as an adjunct professor to teach Global Leadership at the Jack Welch College of Business and Technology in Connecticut, he was not sure if he was qualified for the role. When he prompted the department chair and asked why, out of the hundreds of applicants, she picked him, she mentioned, 'You had this unique combination of global expertise and entrepreneurial experience that we can see you grow and teach even more classes in the future.' Even without formal teaching experience, the collection of experience he had had was the thing that made him stand out in the pile.

What are those experiences that might have mattered? He always knew that he enjoyed teaching. Even presenting at work or giving guest lectures in high schools or colleges, Earl enjoyed being in front of people, especially students. What was more important is that for the specific subject Global Leadership, Earl brought in his experiences travelling in multiple continents to attend the regional

World Economic Forum events, and being able to travel or live in emerging markets like Southeast Asia, Latin America, or Eastern Europe had exposed and enhanced his experiences even further. Oftentimes, we think that travel is not part of our professional experiences, but it could be one of the most important self-education tools that someone can obtain for themselves, immersing in the culture and realizing the cultural differences between geographies.

This also goes to show that each of us have a unique tapestry of life experiences that only we can weave together in our own interesting way, and it's up to us to evaluate where we can potentially shine and build a story around these collections of experiences no matter how small or perceived as irrelevant.

Superpowers Could Be the Main Hiring Filters for VCs and Startups

As founders, executives, and managers, one of the most important functions that you will have is hiring people. People are the lifeblood of your team or your company, so each hire will either make your team great or cause non-stop frustration.

With these somewhat geeky questions, you will automatically be able to determine the following information:

- What are they best in the world at? If they answer the question with conviction, you would know automatically what they are passionate about and may do even in their spare time because they are probably good at it and like the work.
- Are they a complementary fit to the team? Most companies, especially at the beginning, need a specific type of

individual, not just in skills but also in passions, in networks, and in connections. Having to answer this question will help you determine if you fit into the puzzle the team is working to fill in. Sometimes you might be really great, but honestly, you are not just fit for what they need right now.

- Do they strive for global competence? Looking at their previous experiences, either formal or informal ones, having superpowers sometimes means practice, experiences, and a certain consciousness to be the best in the world at something. For example, if they say they love to connect people together, find hints if they have been consistent in getting jobs to sharpen that tool and will weed out candidates that just 'go with the flow'.
- Are they honest with themselves? In a ton of interviews (and in sales), all of us are coached to look at the needs of the other person and 'kind of' customize the message to them. In these questions, you cannot do that because it indicates a sense of self-introspection and a certain self-awareness—the person's strengths and weaknesses—that regardless of the situation or the job, will be the same exact answer no matter what.
- Are they fun? You can obviously change the question to fit what you think is cool. If it was Earl, he is a Marvel fan, so he could ask it a bit differently and not assume everyone liked Superman. It's a fun way to test 'culture-fit' in one question.

Overall, the main point is that for startups and high-performing teams, every person is extremely important. And we are emphasizing 'person' and not what HR says as 'requisition' or project managers refer to as 'resources'. Find a way to hire the best person for the team who fits with not just the skills, but for who they are, what

Now, Discover Your Kryptonite

Equally important to discovering your superpowers is to also figure out what are the things that you are just not good at. Some people call them weaknesses or areas of improvement. No matter what, it is important to mitigate your kryptonites.

When he was a teenager, Billy Price, in what was considered a freak accident, fell three storeys out of a window and found himself paralysed from the chest down in 1996. Over the years, he found workarounds for daily tasks, not being able to walk and having lost the dexterity in his hands. His physical limitations were his kryptonite. Struggling with putting his shoes on for nearly eighteen years, Billy felt like he had to find a way to fix this.

Staring at his feet for a long time, the idea sort of birthed itself. One day, at a Christmas party in 2011 with his childhood friend Darin, an idea with zippers struck Billy and he configured a certain way he could take back his independence.

In 2015, Billy created a shoe with a zipper along the outside and around the toe of each shoe, the upper flap was able to open up and fold completely thus giving the wearer the ability to place their foot onto the inside sole unobstructed. For kids who struggle to tie their shoelaces or for those with disabilities, these shoes made lives easier.

Known as BILLY Footwear, it exists with a mission to provide functional shoes with style. By 2017, Billy was able to get his shoes in Nordstrom, Zappos, and Target.

Turning what was his kryptonite—not being able to put on shoes for himself—into his strength, Billy found his superpower solution: shoes that could be used by those with disabilities.

Billy truly had a passion to build something, even starting as a side hustle that he worked on after his day job at the Federal Aviation Administration (FAA). Eventually, Billy and his partner were making enough sales that they could quit their day jobs.

Finding your kryptonite can be as powerful as finding your superpower. As we mentioned before, a good startup solves real problems, weaknesses in existing structures, so why not start off with yours?

Fill in the blanks: My superpower is _____.
My kryptonite is _____.

11

Real People, Real Relationships: How to Genuinely Build Your Network

'Nice guys may appear to finish last, but usually they are running in a different race.'

—Ken Blanchard

One summer day, Dan was walking in downtown San Francisco on Mission Street after going to the gym. Being an SF native, he tends to do this for fun. He then checked his Google Calendar to see if he had any more meetings on his schedule. He realized that he had registered for a digital health conference where venture capitalists made up the panellists. He didn't know anyone else going to the event and wondered if he should skip it. But as someone who was trying to break into VC at the time, networking was important. Besides, the event was only two blocks away and started in half an hour. He decided that he'd attend the event. Maybe he could sway a chance encounter with an executive into a job or deal flow. After all, there was likely to be free food and drinks and with San Francisco dinners averaging twenty bucks per person, he was sold.

94   Startup Mindsets

Dan arrived at Werqwise on New Montgomery Street ready to learn a thing or two. The panel featured Sean Doolan of Global Founders Capital, Olivia Capra of Kaiser Permanente Ventures, and Amit Garg, the founding partner of a new venture firm called Tau Ventures. The discussion turned out to be pretty educational as they discussed the state of health-tech VCs and startups. Dan learned about the climate for mental health investments and how an exit would be needed to increase venture appetite for funding. When the panel ended, he wanted to meet Amit, but a flock of attendees surrounded the panellists and a line formed. Growing impatient and nudging the urge to walk away, he persisted but Amit had left when he turned away for a second. But the event's networking was still going on and he bumped into an old friend, Eugene, and they drank beers on the house.

The next day, he decided to send Amit a message on LinkedIn saying he enjoyed his talk and had two deals in mental health and cars worth taking a look at. Much to his delight, Amit messaged back in three minutes with his email. He then invited Dan to grab coffee with him in Palo Alto later that week. Dan found it hard to believe that the General Partner of an up-and-coming venture fund had agreed to take a meeting with some kid like him who went to a subpar UC and graduated with an English degree. Two years prior, he had had no idea what venture capital was, let alone how investing in stocks truly worked.

At Verve Coffee Roasters in Palo Alto's University Avenue, Dan and Amit had a great conversation on AI and Tau Venture's thesis and mission on backing applied AI startups. I truly learned a lot from that conversation with Amit, not just about business but how real relationships with real people add value.

Four months later, Dan messaged Amit saying that he had a founder in his network interested in a warm introduction to pitch Tau Ventures their seed round. In his quick fashion, Amit responded and thanked him for considering his venture firm. What happened next is still one of Dan's favourite results from networking. Amit had extended an invitation to Dan and the founder to a private cocktail hour at one of San Francisco's upscale restaurants. Perhaps, this is the fun part of venture capital that no one wants to admit as a venture capitalist. Quality venture networking opportunities are rare and exclusive, invite-only events.

On the night of the event, Dan was a tad nervous but having gone to a ton of networking events as part of Venture University and talking to people about VC was second nature even though he was a broke kid looking for a job at the time. The event was great as he networked with top funds like Norwest; other successful people were in the room as well including Ron Storn, the former Head of People at Lyft, and Joshua Wilson, founder of Tsumobi and part of Y Combinator's first one hundred startups.

The phenomenon of network effects described by NFX, a popular venture firm in Silicon Valley, truly takes place. Real relationships allow for barriers to funding or strategic partnerships to come down. It's these seeds that have the potential to turn into desired results in the future. So, play the long game and keep an open mind. While one meeting and conversation with a potential investor, business partner, or employee can add confidence, you must foster a real relationship if you genuinely want to increase your chance of a desired outcome. Make sure that you are helping the person who you need something from as much as you can. If you want a job, ask yourself how you can make the decision-maker's work easier. If you want funding or resources, don't always make it about you. Instead, take genuine interest in the people you're networking with and then ask them for help.

The truth is, networking events are designed for relationship building and one has to think and feel open-minded about talking to people and building rapport. In addition, being comfortable with oneself and seeing the people in the room as equals makes the whole socializing aspect much easier.

* * *

The Relationship Equation

Have you ever thought of why some of the most meaningful relationships can get built in a three-day retreat but some of your classmates from undergrad, who you saw every day, you don't even remember their names? It might sound geeky, but we've come up with what we call 'The Relationship Equation' to help understand what makes lasting relationships, and it goes something like:

Strength of the relationship = Amplitude × Frequency × Personal relevance

Let's break down the components:

Amplitude: This means how strong or intense the interaction is in a given amount of time. High amplitude activities include a multi-day retreat on an island or a ten-day backpacking trip across Europe or renting an RV and going to Burning Man in the middle of the desert. This typically relays a host of emotions such as excitement, vulnerability, anger, fear, etc. Some of these events are short, but the experience together is so intense that you remember it forever.

On the other side of the spectrum, an example of a low-intensity activities are things that are already routine. Think about it where you go to work every day, going to the same work building. This part doesn't really become as relevant to you and is less memorable because it is a 'normal' interaction.

Frequency: This is defined as how often you interact with the specific person(s) in a given amount of time. High-frequency relationships tend to be with someone you meet on a regular basis.

Think of these people as the ones you might hang out with every weekend or the ones who might stay in the same dorm as you in college. The more often you see and interact with someone, you start to get more familiar with each other.

Personal relevance: This is defined as the type of commonality you have with the specific person. This can also be referred to as the 'connection' that people feel when they meet someone. Typically, high personal relevance could be attributed to a set of common experiences that they have had in their life. Power networks are cultivated when a group of people are bonded by a common interest or a common goal.

Understand that networking is about trying to meet people who care about the ideals you have. Some of them might be social communities or professional communities.

Applying that to cultivating relationships in business and friendships is what takes two people from being complete strangers to two connections willing to work with each other towards a common purpose. Being authentic and a people person goes a lot farther than one may think. Being able to relate to things outside of professional topics brings people closer to each other. It opens up opportunities to show empathy. Friendship is made out of intangibles and the ability to relate deeper than just connecting on the surface level. Once a genuine relationship is established, it's easier to ask for help in business matters.

Frequency in this case was getting coffee with Amit at Verve Coffee in Palo Alto, then suggesting some deals for potential investment. At the time, Tau Ventures was a new fund just getting off the ground so quality deal flow was extremely important. Over time, frequency and amplitude work together to build trust. So, if frequency times amplitude equals trust and trust equals speed then these are the key ingredients in growing any scenario.

Bluedot

People are governed by these notions of what can you do for me, what do you have that can benefit me? As my good friend Jovanni would say, 'They want to know what you can do for them more than what they can do for you.' Approach anybody on the street and expect them to carry a conversation with you and nine times out of ten they'll walk away. However, if you can delight them enough to garner some interest in what you would be able to do for them, you put yourself in a position to get them to help you.

A key example of this happened during spring break of Dan's senior year at UC Riverside. He returned home to San Francisco for a week. After a quarter of rigorous classes and intensive study, he was relieved to have one quarter to go before graduating. He does this thing when he hasn't been home for a while. He goes to downtown SF and walks around. He walks into Golden Gate Taproom, a sports bar near Union Square, to get a drink.

He'll never forget his first experience getting to know a startup CEO. He sat at the bar and ordered a beer on tap. The NBA regular season was coming to a close and March Madness games for college were being played too. Basketball games filled all the screens throughout the bar. The Golden State Warriors were set to play the Memphis Grizzlies and the Final Four of college hoops included University of Florida versus South Carolina.

He could tell a lot of the people in the area were tourists or visiting for the weekend, they just had the out-of-town look, plus there were tons of hotels within walking distance. He noticed a guy sitting to his right, busy on his laptop. It didn't look like he was coding or on a betting website, so Dan was intrigued by what he was doing. You don't see someone on a computer in a bar that often but he guessed that's what San Francisco was becoming.

'What's up, man, you gonna watch the game?' Dan asked to make small talk.

'Hey! Yeah, go Warriors!' the man replied.

Dan immediately noticed his Australian accent.

They exchanged pleasantries and cracked a few jokes he doesn't remember any more.

Eventually, Dan asked, 'What do you do?'

'I run a tech company.'

At the time, Dan was against tech companies and the people who worked for them. He saw tech as the opposite of what he stood for. He became quiet and an expression of disinterest came over him.

Emil offered to get the next round on him. As if he had noticed something. Dan could not not take him up on the offer and the conversation continued. Emil explained that his startup was in the geofences space and that they provided location-based analytics to restaurants and major retailers. When it was time to go, he handed Dan his business card and wished him well in his studies. The card read Emil Davityan, CEO/Founder of Bluedot. Dan didn't see him as a CEO. He realized that no matter what he majored in, English in this case, there was room for anyone to belong in tech and that founders are just people who have extraordinary plans to make the future better.

What started as a random conversation between two folks at a bar became a turning point in the way he perceived the tech industry as a whole. Innovation is now more important than ever and the people who work tirelessly to enrich the lives of people around the world deserve more people who believe in them and their mission.

A lot of getting ahead in an early-stage startup involves asking for favours whether it's intros to potential customers, investors, or trying to become an employee. Many attempts to climb the corporate ladder include jockeying for position and fighting to influence a decision. However, while the amplitude of this connection was strong, Dan made sure to attend one of Bluedot's mini conferences at the office to say hello to Emil and ask for a job. At the time, he was a fresh-out-of-college graduate looking for his first big career break. While he did not end up working for Bluedot, it helped him stay in the picture. It is good to have relationships with CEOs because you never know what will happen in the future.

Fast-forward about two years when he was an analyst for VU Venture Partners in their VC rotational programme, he remembered Emil and sent him an email inquiring about investing in Bluedot's upcoming series B round. Now, he had a chance to provide real value in the form of investment. They had Emil come pitch them the capital raise, and it is still one of his favourite founder–investor meetings to this day. He came to learn that Bluedot helps power location-based marketing allowing brick-and-mortar retailers to understand customers' location-based behaviours. In addition, they also work with East Coast–based EZ passes to allow automatic toll charges for urban governments.

In 2021, Bluedot closed a USD 9 million series B led by Autotech Ventures (investors in Lyft) and, in 2022, it was named among the top fifty most innovative companies by Fast Company,[16] with customers like McDonald's, KFC, and Dunkin' Donuts opting to use their geolocation technology to enable faster food pickups for customers. 'We're able to detect the exact moment when the customer enters the drive-through or the curbside pickup area, or when they walk into the store,' explained co-founder and CEO Emil Davityan during a *Startup Mindsets* podcast interview. Bluedot's product suite, Tempo, which launched in 2020, tracks a customer's location, alerting staff to prepare food at the optimal time.

What started as many long nights of working on research and development and building their main product, a software

---

[16] Judy Chan, 'Bluedot Named to Fast Company's Most Innovative List 2022', Bluedot, 8 March 2022, https://bluedot.io/blog/fast-companys-most-innovative-company-list-2022/.

development kit, has blossomed into a venture backed startup providing retailers essential customer data around the physical behaviours of consumers to deliver one-of-a-kind notifications. Along the journey, Emil recalls hundreds of conversations with VCs who rejected their idea and told them, 'It's never going to work out, good luck.' But Emil persevered, moved from Sydney, Australia, to San Francisco to launch an office in the US. Bluedot was a capital-intensive business desperate for venture funding in order to build the product further and scale the team.

Plug and Play

In 2005, Silicon Valley was recovering from the first tech bubble bursting. Three hundred thousand people had lost their jobs, thus creating tons of empty office space in Palo Alto, Mountain View, and along the 101 freeway. Saeed Amidi called his business partner, Jojo Flores, to tell him that there may be an opportunity to purchase real estate for bargain prices. Jojo conducted some initial research to find out that there was 10 million square feet of empty office space.

The pair originally ran a water bottle company named Wilkins and used their profits to purchase real estate in the Palo Alto area. What became home to the first non-garage office of Google, PayPal, Logitech, and a company called Danger founded by Andy Rubin, the CEO of Android (acquired by Microsoft), for USD 500 million also earned the nickname the 'Lucky Building' because high-performing startups emerged from the offices. Located a block away from Stanford University's campus, 165 University Avenue was a building that Jojo and Saeed first purchased and leased to startups.

Aside from the real estate business, the Amidi family also owned the rug store Medallion Rugs, located just down the block from the lucky building. One of the first marketing activities Jojo conducted to promote the space was to make Medallion Rugs into a rendezvous location for venture capitalists and potential employees to get to know startups in the space.

At one point, Plug and Play had amassed relationships with 700 venture capitalists around the Valley. Social events at the rug store was how they met Ron Conway, one of the most influential angel investors; Tim Draper; and Sequoia Capital, the world's most well-known venture firm known for investments in Google, YouTube, Airbnb, and many other well-known startups. The venture capitalists and the team at Plug and Play had an agreement to curate startups and the VCs would come to Plug and Play once a year to take a look at the startups. This eventually became an accelerator to help startups looking for funding get mentorship and work within a community.

Jojo told the VCs, 'If you have any startups that want new office space, please come to us. And by the way, if you want to take a look, we have some startups in the building that could use funding.'

It eventually turned into a programme and Jojo hired a team to be on the venture side.

Jojo and his business partner, Saeed, had the idea to rent office space to small teams and it became the first model for co-working. At the same time, they realized they could scale the investment activities they had and it gave them a chance to see other opportunities in the market. This became Plug and Play Tech Center.

Today, Plug and Play is known as Silicon Valley in a box with a global presence including offices in Singapore and Indonesia.

Plug and Play is a venture fund that invests without having raised their own fund. They fund the investments through cash flows from their corporate business portal and curate startups for corporations across the world. What started as a stint in the plastics resin industry morphed into a real estate business that housed prominent technology companies at their infancy. But Plug and Play saw opportunities to bridge entrepreneurs within their office space with venture capitalists and corporations who would benefit greatly from the technology invented within their walls. While the value of office space could have been enough, Jojo and Saeed decided to go outside of their niche and invest in startups while making connections with venture capitalists to share deal flow.

Five Hacks to Build Your Trusted Network

From Dan's experience talking to many sources and surveying entrepreneurs, he listed down a couple of the top activities or 'hacks' to grow your own personal network of contacts and build long-lasting friendships over time. He challenges you, the reader, to make sure to keep these personal key metrics in order to cultivate a relationship model that will sustain through the years:

- Speak in at least ten events per calendar year. Whether you're an introvert or extrovert, practise talking about your project and flex your ability to teach in multiple projects.
- Host or create your own event at least once a year. It is important for you to create your own event in an area where you want to grow your branding or expertise.
- Join or create your own curated network based on your background or personal passion. It is imperative to start or join a curated networking group where you might be able to create relationships small or large because you know them beyond the newspaper.
- Do at least ten unconditional favours for your existing business partners in a year. This is key. Have you kept in touch over the years? This is a way for you to reciprocate all the favours.
- Build contacts in every part of the ecosystem—from follow-on funds to experts or service providers.

Overall, the message is to build 'real relationships' that you can keep in touch with and never skip a beat. If a person's network is their net worth, then why not make sure to always cultivate it? There are so many unregimented/non-linear processes for success, it's necessary to be open-minded and proactive in the startup industry. Connections are everything when properly utilized. They unlock doors that would normally be closed.

12

Communication: Sharing Your Story

'There's always room for a story that can transport people to another place.'
—J.K. Rowling

Martin Luther King talking about his dream for an equitable America. John F. Kennedy's moon shot speech. The way that Franklin Roosevelt handled the bombing of Pearl Harbor as the day that will live in infamy. All of these moments are captured in our memories and the moments of time. Everyone and everything has its own story from when it started to how it is going. While these were monumental events in history, known for their significance, there is just as much significance to the individual who decides to pick up the pen and craft their own journey in building a business. In this chapter, we will examine how successful entrepreneurs have been able to optimize for personal brand narrative by scaling a digital presence through honesty and transparency.

A digital story is the same as casting a net into the ocean and fishing. Finding your first 1,000 followers promotes social growth and the goodwill of the company. The more people resonate with what you are building, the more doors will open for creating

106 Startup Mindsets

goodwill and a future fan base that will show their support and externally validate you for the next thousand fans.

According to an article from Boston University,[17] over 75 per cent of adults have a fear of public speaking or, as medical experts call it, glossophobia. According to the article, 'Those who suffer from glossophobia tend to experience the classic fight or flight response when speaking in front of a group, even if the group only consists of a few people. They may tremble, sweat, freeze, and so on. As their brains release adrenaline and steroids, their blood sugar levels and heart rates increase. The symptoms are not necessarily limited to a public speaking event; they can also happen prior to the event, that is, when it is anticipated. While glossophobic people may know that this fear is irrational, they have the least amount of power in controlling their feelings.'

While many of us associate sharing our story with being on stage and giving a public speech like these historical icons, today's technology and media landscape has greatly given many people more options for garnering interactions with viewers. Even twenty years ago, there were only three channels in order to get the word out that you exist—TV, radio, and print. Today, there are a multitude of tools from the type of social media like Facebook, LinkedIn, TikTok, and X (formerly Twitter), among other niche players such as Clubhouse and Twitch. Also, the form is very different now, from sixty-second snippets on Instagram to a well-written blog that can be consumed in five minutes to an hour-long podcast and a recorded YouTube lecture, it's up to you what form or channel you want to have in order to tell your story.

Now you may be asking, what is so important about my personal story in how it relates to creating a company? Or why not just focus on product and business operations? In today's interconnected society, we all get our news through digital mediums such as Facebook and Twitter, which are usurping

---

[17] 'What Is Glossophobia?' *The Nerve Blog*, 27 November 2017, http://sites.bu.edu/ombs/2017/11/27/what-is-glossophobia/.

Communication: Sharing Your Story 107

network television. It is also no secret that the feeling economy is garnering attention. As more people express themselves on digital mediums like LinkedIn, TikTok, Instagram, or YouTube, the general public is watching content that is unscripted and authentic like never before. In a digital era that demands speed and perfection, people crave real connections to other people.

In 2020, whole families, from grandparents to grandchildren, posted TikTok videos of themselves dancing, which created new trends and became viral instantly. With the need to connect with followers and build a brand, both personal and professional, utilizing organic social reach can build an audience to sell to.

The value of putting your business' story out tells the public what you stand for. Stories are powerful when others emotionally resonate. With the likelihood of already existing competitors claiming to do your job better, people need an X factor. Otherwise, it's like all these brands of soap are the same. For example, Old Spice has a commercial that featured an attractive male provocatively claiming that using Old Spice caters to attracting women. Within thirty days of the launch of the campaign, Old Spice saw over 40 million views on YouTube, and a 107 per cent increase in body wash sales.[18] But that's the large consumer packaged goods marketing attempt. When you're a founder on demo day and you're pitching investors new ideas, create content that resonates with that niche audience.

Building Your Personal Brand and Leveraging LinkedIn and TikTok

In 2018, after graduating UC Riverside with a degree in Finance, founder of Wonsulting, Jonathan Javier, found his passion:

---

[18] Transformation Marketing Admin, 'Marketing Campaign Success – Old Spice', Transformation Marketing, 20 April 2015, https://www. transformationmarketing.com/marketing-campaing-success-old-spice/.

utilizing the power of LinkedIn to help students and prospective applicants from non-targeted universities get into their dream careers at dream companies. The truth is, employers tend to hire from top-tier universities leaving non-traditional applicants with harder hills to climb in getting into their dream career. Especially with entry-level job applications demanding two years of experience when the majority of students just have degrees.

Jonathan made an unconventional—and what would be deemed as vulnerable—post about how he did not get an offer from Google until his third try. While it would be easy to gloat about just getting into Google, he did not, choosing instead to focus on his process of overcoming adversity. The post garnered 45,000 reactions and 2,000 comments, many from people he had never met before.

Jonathan successfully elevated his personal brand by appealing to the shared experience of being rejected from a job but then curating his content to be empowering to his followers.

Truly communicating failures and shortcomings, all things that would be under the iceberg of success, allow your audience to find things that resonate from your story to theirs, thus allowing a connection and a brand that's more than colours and words. Brand is an emotion that people get when they see your name and company. To evoke such emotions is an art and practice that comes with consistency and good content.

Wonsulting grew its follower count on the LinkedIn page from 1,500 to 8,000 in two months then from 8,000 to 15,000 in half the time. The power of network effects and a bias for action propelled their growth. Today, Wonsulting is successful because they communicate their story and mission to turn underdogs into winners loud and proud. The next time you want to post something on your social network, think: Does this connect with my audience in a unique way, and does it share what I am about?

During the pandemic, Jonathan would post every day on TikTok strategies and tips for landing a job, whether it was interview tips

Communication: Sharing Your Story 109

like answering in a STAR method (situation, task, action, result) or literal responses he sent back as thank you notes to the interviewers. The consistency ultimately galvanized his brand and he was able to leave Cisco because of the income he was making from brand deals and consulting job seekers to work on Wonsulting full time.

One evening, as Besnik Bajrami was grabbing dinner with a few co-workers at JP Morgan's Manhattan office, they started bouncing ideas off of each other.

'Hey, we're managing the assets of millionaires and the ultra-rich, who is doing this for our family?'

Everyone looked at each other in the room in curiosity. It was a valid point.

'Gosh, for a financial adviser to even speak to someone, they've got to have a minimum fifty thousand in the bank.'

To explore what other people who wouldn't be biased thought, Bez went to a business networking event in Hell's Kitchen after work one day and asked what people thought of this idea that would provide regular people who couldn't afford a financial adviser with an investment adviser as part of a premium monthly subscription model. The feedback was overwhelming in that they would be interested in it.

What started as an idea for an Instagram page that would attract would-be customers began with posts of skyscrapers in Manhattan asking simple finance questions and suggestions like 'Do you know what a bond is?' 'Treat the hundred-dollar client the same as the million-dollar client, they're the same people to you.'

When deciding to leave JP Morgan to pursue starting his own company, Bez was leaving a USD 100,000 salary with an almost guaranteed promotion to go all-in on an idea he had that was not producing any cash at the time. Six months after leaving JP Morgan, he found himself stuck and unable to turn the corner on monetizing a newsletter with a team who had success in monetizing other ventures in the past.

Launched in August of 2018, Cube Wealth is a subscription service that provides education and mentorship for retail investors. Utilizing a Slack group chat, Bez provides research reports on markets, stocks, and business advice for a community sourced by running an Instagram page that provides market updates and discussions on investing.

It took a year and three months after leaving JP Morgan's Investment Banking division to hit profitability. Anyone who believes that being able to monetize a product or service overnight is easy has underestimated the job description. The mindset of yearning for the freedom to operate on your own terms, when you want, how you want, and at the same time being in love with doing what you're doing despite not making much money from it takes unbelievable fortitude.

Communicating your personal story and building a brand around your company can be daunting and a tough task to handle. But if there's a constant positive to putting yourself out there, it's that people don't buy what you do, they buy WHY you do it. For Bez Bajrami, it was because he saw that there are so many people who want to learn how to invest but don't know where to start and can get misled by constant get-rich schemes like Bitcoin or forex. For Jonathan, it was knowing the pain of putting your all into a job interview and getting rejected and wanting to get those applicants over the hump.

Sharing your story matters, whether it is your personal journey as an employee-turned-founder or as a new idea that becomes a company that needs its first thousand fans. Jonathan realized he had a passion for enabling underdog applicants in their dream careers.

Bez realized that no one was helping those interested in learning about investing, so he began putting out content that engaged new investors such as the *Cube Podcast* and weekly live streams on Twitch. Communication can be as simple as a LinkedIn post that announces what you are building or getting featured in a

Communication: Sharing Your Story

blog or newspaper that highlights what you are doing. Ultimately, public relations is how products find people and vice versa when startups are just beginning. The good news is now it is easier than ever to reach audiences and resonate organically without advertisement spend.

It is not uncommon, talking to strangers is indeed in decline because of the pandemic and having our noses in phones 24/7. But not succumbing to our apprehensions and doing what makes us uncomfortable is where progress takes place. It is difficult especially because we value comfort and turning off that voice in your head doesn't quite work every time.

Vulnerability Breeds Empathy

The thing VCs care about is being confident enough to make an investment in your business so that it will return their entire fund value or more. That's literally the main purpose of venture capital. They have pressure from their limited partners to generate returns. On ABC's *Shark Tank* season 19, an entrepreneur from Chicago Nick Sky came on the show to pitch how his company, Changed, would contribute to solving the student loan crisis in America. As of September 2023, there are 1.74 trillion in existing student loan payments.[19]

At the time, Nick revealed to the sharks that he was driving Uber in the morning and late afternoons to pay the bills while the company was doing a measly USD 800 in revenue. It was in this moment of vulnerability that revealed the grit and how much his idea meant to him.

Dan and Nick managed to raise USD 250,000 from Mark Cuban in exchange for 25 per cent of equity.

---

[19] Eliza Haverstock and Anna Helhoski, 'Student Loan Debt Statistics: 2024', Nerdwallet, 5 February 2024, https://www.nerdwallet.com/article/loans/student-loans/student-loan-debt.

Sharing your story may not come easy but it is one way to convey the present reality that your business needs help and those listening are more inclined to help once they see that they can be of value. When we are comfortable with how we perceive our lives are turning out and believe in the path we are on, we see ourselves as the lead character, more inclined to act towards a favourable future.

13

Constant Reflection: What Matters to You and Why?

'I love those who can smile in trouble, who can gather strength from distress, and grow brave by reflection.' Tis the business of little minds to shrink, but they whose heart is firm, and whose conscience approves their conduct, will pursue their principles unto death.'

—Leonardo da Vinci

Stanford Graduate School of Business is one of the most selective MBA schools in the world, boasting an admission rate typically in the 6 to 8 per cent range. With an alumni roster such as Phil Knight, the founder of Nike, or Charles Schwab, the founder of the investment house that bears his name, there are many amazing business leaders who came out of the halls of this school in the heart of Silicon Valley.

What is ironic is that the admission essay to this elite business school is nothing about spreadsheets, investments, stocks, or even people management. It actually has nothing to do directly with business, it goes straight to the heart of the individual. Their essay, which has been the same for many years, asks one simple question: 'What matters to you most and why?' This simple yet thought-provoking question is the foundation for many years of self-reflection and personal thought. It is important to keep reflecting and take a pause to answer life's many important questions.

Just a background that maybe not everyone knows: Earl had applied to Stanford three times before his MBA application— first for undergrad transfer for engineering, second for a PhD in engineering, and a last one for a masters in engineering. All rejected.

So, in 2006, Earl applied to Stanford Graduate School of Business by accident and without much hope. They announced that for the first time in the history of the school, they would experiment to admit students who did not take the GMAT, but would accept people who have taken only the GRE. For most B-school hopefuls, GMAT is the prerequisite to applying for any programme—a make it or break it exam. He had the GRE because he had to take it for his application in 2004 for his masters at Cornell for engineering and re-used his scores that were dismal, it was 760 in math and 400 in verbal in the GRE. For people not familiar, the highest score is 800 for each. He had done fine in math, but he was in the 30th percentile in verbal, think of it that 70 per cent of ALL applicants had a higher score than him.

Thinking that this was a long shot, he wrote the admission essays within a span of three weeks in the plane on the way to and from Washington DC when he was on a business trip for Raytheon Company where he was working as a systems engineer at their space and airborne systems division. The unconventional and surprising theme of the essays—'Partying like a rockstar.'

After a couple of months of sending in the application, he got an email saying that he had an interview with an angel investor named Dave Witherow. The interview was to take place at the Starbucks coffee shop in Santa Monica Beach in Los Angeles. Dave was an entrepreneur and sold his company to Dow Jones. He told Earl that he would wear jeans and a leather jacket and

Constant Reflection: What Matters to You and Why? 115

not to be more overdressed than him. After their conversation, Earl's view of business changed forever and he fell in love with the school a bit more—that business can be kind, informal, and authentic.

In a few weeks, he got a call from a Palo Alto number, a call from Derek Bolton, the admissions director of the GSB, congratulating him on being admitted to the class of 2009. Five years after graduation during his visit to the Philippines, Derek confirmed that Earl was the first, if not one of the first admits in the history of the GSB, never to take the GMAT. He started in Stanford as a bright-eyed engineer trying to learn about business, despite not even taking a single finance or accounting course in college. At that time, his peers weren't owners of startups or venture funds and didn't have billionaire classmates yet, and no big fancy corporate titles. It was an environment where everyone was equal—all were students and eventually friends.

There is a sense of anxiousness not because he would compare himself to the accomplishments of his classmates, but more so, how he would compare himself to the dream he set out to achieve when he applied and committed to his stated mission when he attended Stanford MBA school. He vividly remembers on the first day of MBA school, the head of admissions challenged the class—'You've been selected, what will you do to help make an impact on the world?' Then the dean iterated the mission of the school—'Change lives, change organizations, and change the world; and you all can change the world'—instilling the belief that you indeed, in your lifetime, can change the world.

As part of this book, Earl has reproduced his admission essay here, verbatim, even with grammatical errors, to remind him and the world of what his dreams were when he was twenty-four and for the world to hold him accountable to stay true and authentic to this dream. With an open heart and at the risk of being vulnerable here it is:

Essay A: What matters most to you, and why?

Three months ago, I got to see Bono, the lead singer of U2, give a speech in Dallas about the problems in Africa and he said something so profound that it really made me think. He said, 'We as citizens of the world need to solve the problem of global poverty – because poverty leads to the elimination of hope, without hope there is despair, in your despair you will commit crime, and with the natural evolution of crime is in terrorism.' Wow… if only all of us in the world eliminated the human nature of selfishness then the world would be a better place. Since I was young, my parents exposed me to the harsh realities of poverty.

Growing up in the Philippines, a country at which 90% of its population is below the poverty line, I was exposed to this fact everyday – and being part of the upper 10%, it is easy to shun away and ignore this fact, but something inside me always said that 'Your life should have meaning and it's your obligation to give back.' Who do you want to be when you die? If you had a chance to inspire the common person to try to be future leaders and dream more than they are right now, wouldn't you want a chance to do this?

Over the past months in my quest to answer my quarter life crisis, I have tried to answer the basic questions regarding 'what is my purpose in life? What is the meaning of living?' Throughout my soul searching, I have looked and reflected on my past, tried to look for who I want to be, and what is important to me. While reading the classic book 'Good to Great', Collins talked about the hedgehog concept – which is, in his words, how a company or an individual can be great. The 3 things are: what drives your economic engine, are you the best at what you do, and

Constant Reflection: What Matters to You and Why?

what is your passion? This struck me, often thinking… of yes… what is my passion? I had to dig deep and look at my core values – the things that really really matter to me.

While in a career planning session at Raytheon, I wrote down my four main values: the pursuit of excellence, seeing the world and party like a rock star, having a lasting impact in everything you touch, and making the world a better place.

As of now, my core mission is in helping educate and create a dream for young people who might not have had a dream before. My personal belief is that education is the great equalizer, where in a university, it is really not how much money you have but rather what is in your head and how to use this potential to create more opportunities to uplift yourself and your family. As of now, I am a true believer of the mentoring process. I realize that when talking to people younger than you, you have to be careful of what you say or do. Why is that? Because every word and every action you do can impact someone's life forever. I personally am involved in trying to be a mentor, not just through being a Big Brother, but more so to my peers and younger or older folks that may need some guidance in life or their careers. I enjoy giving career talks and advice to middle school and HS students, and also would never shun away a conversation from any student that asks for my advice. I am always involved in such activities as career panel discussions or giving a leadership talk, but what I really enjoy is having a one-on-one with someone and just trying to inspire and get them to have goals in life to reach. I was also fortunate to be invited to sponsor five less fortunate students to shoulder their high school tuition in the Philippines, and why not? I had a chance to meet them, and some of them are single moms, or taxi cab drivers, or waiters, and just seeing the tears in their eyes when they found that their USD 200 tuition was covered, touched me a lot. For some of us, we take education for granted, some of us believe that it's a right for every citizen of the world to get, but for most of the world, it is a privilege. If only I can make the world a better place by helping more people get the opportunities that I have been luckily presented with, I will do that.

So knowing my core mission, how does this tie into one of my values of excellence. I have to admit though that I am not this super organized person that has his palm pilot always on, pristine office desks, or nice pressed clothes... but the excellence that I am talking about is deeper... beyond physical... it lies with ambition. I love just 'believing' in the future and who will be and will become 'one day.' Maybe this is one of my weaknesses, that I sometimes get frustrated at people who 'just want to be an ordinary worker.'

I truly believe that all of us can be extraordinary. As one passage said... 'It is better to be hot or cold than to be lukewarm.' I believe that only when you have this drive or ambition always burning inside you, then you will always stay positive. We live in a cynical world... always people who try to put people down. I believe that with this common cause of uplifting people from poverty through education... you should have the core fire of trying to lift people to great new heights.

I have to admit, my goal is to be CEO of a Global 100 company in 15 years. Why? It is not based on a hunger for greed or power... but it's because of the opportunity. When you are in a position, you have influence in more countries than one, and having the respect and leverage of an institution to back up your cause – you can truly make a macro level impact. I believe that I could create a win-win situation at which the corporation would be able to be recognized as a great global corporate citizen and be able to have more kids go through school. My goal is to be a Warren Buffet or a Bill Gates – great corporate thought leaders – but adheres to the values of education and social responsibility. I believe that their example has inspired me that true leaders are indeed true givers – and I would want to be like them in the future.

Lastly, and on a lighter note, one of my core values is to 'party like a rockstar.' Although I may not be good at instruments, I believe that my life can always be a constant song at which each day is another song to be written on. I am a big believer in crazy parties and in traveling the world. I realize that these are some of the few times that you are real – you usually laugh a lot, dance like you don't care, and being able to just be you. This translates into being me. Sometimes I feel that I am the most transparent guy that people would talk to. I usually tell people what I'm thinking and try not to have any hidden agenda at all. I get irritated by people who have these agendas in mind, and are always putting on a façade to reach the next career step. I treat life as it is... and usually try to put on a smile all the time. The one advice that one of my mentors in Florida told me before I left is 'the trick to making it to the top is to always keep a positive attitude.' I realize that although people can try to fake people positively, it is not the voice tone or the choice of words that make the difference, but more so, your 'aura' will just be there.

Travel is also one big thing on my list. I really believe that the world is so big, so interesting, so many places to go to, that a lifetime is too short to see it all. Why is travel, particularly to a foreign land, so big for me? I think this is one of the greatest leadership training that one will ever get. I went to Prague last year, not knowing what it looks like and how to get from the airport to the hostel, and not knowing anyone at all. I realize that everything in life is like this... uncertain of the future. But like me, and I am still alive now and back in the US, the only way to learn something new is to take risks. I believe leaders are people who don't settle for the status quo and people who are willing to risk their lives or careers for something they truly believe in. Also, in traveling, you get to learn. As what the Japanese Minister of Education told my dad when he was doing graduate school in Japan said 'if you love your kids, make them travel.' I totally agree because you would be able to learn about so many cultures, see so much history and meet very interesting people. For example, I learned from a traveler, that people in Denmark usually 'kick out' their sons and daughters for 2 months when they turn 16. They expect them to travel to other countries, at a minimum go around Europe, try to live on odd jobs, and stay in hostels. This culture recognized something fundamental early on: that travel is a great maturing process for their youth.

I think that I can sum up what matters to me in one word… DREAM. I believe that by helping people to dream by being a mentor or creating a scholarship for them or by holding on to your own dreams and keeping a positive attitude and taking good risks will create better and future leaders for our truly global world and will shape to create a brighter and better future for the generations to come.

As Earl read his essay again, he felt a sense of pride that he had been honest to himself and his principles despite all the changes and challenges in life. This reinforces his belief that if you spend many hours on deep reflection and try to find your true self, then you might discover the inner core that drives your reason for being. It is impossible to know with certainty whether our actions will generate the outcomes we desire. In fact, nowadays, it is more difficult to land a job, secure funding, and build a successful startup.

Constant Reflection: What Matters to You and Why? 121

A lot of our pursuits have been in limbo, especially during a global pandemic. However, just because statistics and prior failures may not influence us to be optimistic, there is no reason to not dream. If you know you have a good direction and you know people who can help you reach that objective, you should go for it. Having an entrepreneurial mindset is being okay not knowing what is going to happen and still moving forward. Because there is always the unpredictability factor that goes against convention and at the end of the day operating like a startup involves risk.

During Dan's time interning for Venture University, a new concept that combines working for a venture capital fund and being taught at the same time by venture capitalists, a common mantra he abided by was the statement, 'You should have done it yesterday,' in relation to everything that had to do with the job, which was often analysing startups, sending outreach emails, etc. There was this energy in the room that he'll never forget in the short four months of working there—the idea that we needed to close an investment deal before the end of the programme. This notion that time was scarce and work was the only thing in our way of reaching this end goal captivated us and made his cohort work twice as hard. We looked everywhere for startups that we perceived could provide good exit opportunities in the future. Indeed, this is the overarching purpose of a venture fund, to generate sizable returns for its limited partners who made the fund possible in the first place. Now, that is not to say a VC can't be all for partnering with founders and being the resource they need to expand their businesses.

Whether the five investments we made as a cohort succeed or fail, Dan's time wearing the venture capitalist hat will always be memorable. It provided a first-row seat to the entrepreneurs daring to leave an indelible mark on the world and the opportunity to support their dreams with capital, advice, and an ear willing to listen.

14

Overcoming Obstacles

'You stop taking risks when you start thinking you have something to lose.'
—Dheeraj Pandey, founder of Nutanix

Doing anything special tends to involve some sort of risk whether it is not meeting the long-term expectations we set out for ourselves or the subtle concern of feeling ashamed or out of place from risking financial situations or relationships. High aspirations in the context of startups are engulfed with external and internal challenges that do not get solved overnight most of the time. Things like realizing the problem you want to create a solution for, finding the right people to do it with, closing customers and investors are at the helm of the young startup experience. But perhaps, we are acting in the best interest of preserving our ego when we self-reject because we don't want to experience being let down. It is impossible to focus on the fact that you are solving customers' problems all the time when operating a business requires you to do so many different things. Yes, a mission helps, of course, but one needs to act in the company's best interest and not one's own.

A journey loses its significance without roadblocks—both physical and emotional. Obstacles serve as tests to help us truly determine whether or not we want something. We quickly learn if

'X' is worth the efforts of 'Y' and what efforts are needed in 'Y' in order to achieve 'X'.

In fact, it is almost difficult to envision the word 'journey' without the connotation of difficulty along the way. A journey is travelling from one place to another. Dan was stuck with the image of travelling across a desert or crossing an ocean. In entrepreneurship, the journey is watching an idea grow into a product, generating revenue, and scaling a team to make the wheels turn. In relationships, a journey starts from the moment you meet someone to the point that they are friends and you share special moments with each other.

But what makes a journey truly a journey are these things we love to hate—obstacles, either physical or mental hurdles that stand in the way of a perceived desire. Small startups commonly begin with funds raised from angel investors, friends and family rounds, or VCs, ensuring there's enough capital to keep the business afloat, then use that capital to fuel innovation, find the right customer and sell to them or build a solution that people will want to use time and time again. There's an internal doubt that comes into question when founders hear their business being degraded and passed on, the cash in the bank low, and each day becoming harder to operate.

Victory in this field comes down to how many intelligent risks you are willing to take. It would be impossible to create something groundbreaking without pushing the frontiers of innovation and challenging the status quo. Although common knowledge suggests it is easier for us to do what is safe with certainty, moments arrive to challenge this thinking. In a startup environment, the company will never grow without taking the risk of hurting your ego. Achieving these objectives requires perseverance, and what they don't tell you is that in order for high aspirations to come to fruition, failure is part of the equation. It is by constantly iterating to deliver the best product, the best sales demo, the best marketing campaign, the best . . . you get the point.

Overcoming Obstacles 125

Amid the hectic lifestyle that comes with operating a startup, remember why you started and it serves you well to remain mission-driven towards the reality you hope your product can create. When people are motivated by things like fame and fortune, all direct results of a successful tenure doing something in relation to this field, all you get is that. History has taught us that people are called to work extremely hard for something and can sustain the energy needed to do so because it is their goal to improve every day and vastly improve the lives of those who will benefit from the solution.

Building a Startup to Transform the Philippines

It was late in 2019 when Earl decided to help start a company with his classmate from Stanford that focused on bringing a massive change in the financial services industry in emerging markets, starting with his home country, the Philippines. They had this idea that if they could use data and technology the right way, they could unlock the potential of millions if not billions of the next generation of human beings who might not have been given access to formal financial services because the old system was optimized to serve the top 5 per cent globally and not to spread the opportunity to the remaining 95 per cent. Not knowing that a few months later, one of the most devastating humanitarian, health, and economic crises would hit the world, they would have never known that the next twelve to eighteen months would be the biggest test in our career—to start building a company from scratch during a time when the world was changing very quickly, not for the better, but the worst.

As Earl writes today, only one word probably exhibits the spirit of many of his peers who are starting or pushing through building companies that try to solve large, difficult, systemic problems during a time when their personal and professional job securities are at risk daily: it would be the word '**conviction**'.

126 Startup Mindsets

For entrepreneurs, conviction is often seen as the will to move forward despite overwhelming odds. I am sure that most of us know the story of David versus Goliath, or the battle of the 300, or maybe Frodo and the Lord of the Rings. Conviction for most startup entrepreneurs is deeply rooted in achieving a world-changing idea because we fundamentally believe that if we are successful, the world will be better with this technology being utilized. It is also the driving force for founders that despite the hundreds of rejections from potential partners and customers to try the product or the thousands of noes they receive from investors, they still find the spark to not give up and get discouraged.

Conviction is a term that most venture capitalists talk about while considering the decision if they would like to invest in a startup. As investors, many meetings, data points, and discussions are pointed towards answering the questions, 'Do we have enough conviction to invest in this deal?' The venture capital industry, despite funding scalable companies, still has unscalable decision-making processes, often relying on human logic and emotions before they decide to invest. Can the committee of venture partners decide without a shadow of a doubt that out of the thousands of deals that they could put money into, this would be one of the few that they would put their careers on the line for?

For the first eighteen months of building a startup between 2020 and 2022, Earl had many moments of fear and doubt that he had to overcome both on the personal and professional side—whether it be delays in product launch because they needed to cross one more regulatory hurdle or seeing the stock market drop his life savings while having no income coming in and worrying if his family has enough if an unexpected medical bill arises or do they have enough runway to make it to their next milestone to raise the next round of funding. These are many points where he just had to have faith to keep on pushing despite overwhelming pressures as a founder and as a father. During this time, he had many thoughts—*What if I had a stable job to ride out the pandemic?*

Overcoming Obstacles

Or maybe I am not cut out to be a founder? Or should I find a backup plan if this thing does not pan out?

It seems that every time he got into these modes of desperation, glimmers of hope started to show up. Whether it is an unexpected support programme from the government or a milestone met that unlocks another source of funding or an acceptance in supportive communities like the OnDeck, Techstars, or StartX that gives you the network to keep you focused and help accelerate your startup goals or a VC that decides to cut you a cheque to increase your runway by another twelve to eighteen months—these things balanced out the hard times that he faced and made him realize that moments of desperation are sweeter when overcoming these is celebrated later on.

Looking back, in the past eighteen months, he had to always ask himself, 'Why am I doing this?' When times are tough, the answer that comes to mind is the reason why we chose to start a company, and most entrepreneurs decide to do it not because hard problems are easy for them to solve but because a group of idealistic, crazy people risked a lot to give a chance to make the world a little bit better if they are successful.

He is very optimistic that he will find amazing entrepreneurs and ideas coming out of this pandemic economy that has overcome many near-death experiences, and still found a way to survive in this environment. He is also excited for the investors who are taking bold investing risks at this time and not retreating to a conservative 'wait and see' approach but are backing promising early startup companies that are tackling not just the needs of today, but the potential game-changing ideas that will impact the world, not just next year, but in the next five, seven, and ten years when the memory of the pandemic is over.

Although the result of his ventures is still unknown and may succeed or fail, he knows that no setback, even at a scale of a global pandemic, will make him change his conviction that if he is successful, they have a real chance to unlock the human potential of millions if not billions in emerging markets, and he is grateful to have a chance to do this when the world might need it the most.

You come back from these meetings that don't go your way, you do really well but just not well enough to unlock the access. It feels like a lost cause and insanity to move forward because going through the process again will hurt. During Plentina's seed round, there were hundreds of rejections from investors to business partners to customers. But the leaf eventually turned and they were able to raise USD 2.2 million in seed capital. This took longer than expected.

Failure Gives Success its Flavour

Society frames failure and coming up short in an unnecessarily negative way. We are trained to see only the tip of the iceberg and crave the feeling of being on top of the world too often. Moments like getting your dream job then posting about it on LinkedIn or some major accolade. It is not our fault that we think this way. There is not exactly someone to point the finger at, but social media has forced us to be competitive in unhealthy ways. 'Oh so and so just bought a brand new car, I know this because he posted about it all over Instagram and it got 200 likes.' Now I should want to buy a new car too, that way I can feel validated about my life. This leads to rat race thinking, which places you against imaginary competitors. This is also a contributing factor to poor self-esteem and bad mental health. Instead, it is better to run your own race, one that appeals to your individual circumstances.

Picture spending your free time on the couch just scrolling through Instagram and seeing your friends doing better than you because they are smiling and out and about with other people. Or the amount of likes they get is higher than what you got. Today's youth are undergoing challenges prior generations never dealt with.

Coming back to running a business, we tailor our expectations to what others with similar backgrounds to ours have achieved. 'Oh so and so went to this school, earned this degree and now works at this company.' I think I can achieve similar results because I work hard and share the same interests. While this works out in a lot of instances, most of the time it does not. Are we supposed to feel like we underachieved? Heck no!

Applying a mindset of 'I am not entitled to anything and my motivation to further my business comes from an external source not necessarily what is immediately in front of me will serve me better in the long run.

The amazing feeling of success comes from doing things that you weren't sure you were capable of. A popular perception of achievement is that the result is the only thing that matters.

But there's success in bouncing back from discouraging rejection. When Earl first started the *Startup Mindsets* podcast, he thought it would be easy to record himself talking. Pressing Record and talking into a microphone is not that difficult but he was conscious and insecure about how he sounded. *Did I stutter too often, why was I saying 'um' in every sentence, what if people think my voice sounds awkward?*

Whitney Sales, the general partner at Forum Ventures, an early-stage software as a service startup accelerator, said when mentoring founders in a batch: 'You can't be ashamed. It's your job to hold the value of your product. Be proud of what you put out because you're always going to think it can be better, salespeople will always think it can be better, your engineers will always think that it can be better. You kind of just need to get past it.'

In reality, the word 'rejection' is just information. Taking it personally is giving it more power than you need to, making yourself feel bad.

You don't need to pay your dues. Just ask like you deserve it. Think about how far you have come and what once existed that no longer is a challenge for you any more or how you think differently about doing arduous tasks because you stuck it out long enough. I'm sure there are times of triumph and relief because those things were truly hard. Obstacles mainly exist because we lack the most suitable approach to navigate that obstacle. It may take a full six months to fundraise a round or close a customer. But those noes only help you examine your previous beliefs about, 'Do I still want to do this?' One of the main benefits of being persistent in arduous processes is that it eventually becomes easier over time. No one becomes an excellent programmer overnight or gains the experience of a seasoned salesperson, marketer, or any important company function either.

Figure out what obstacles stand in your way—mental obstacles like feeling ashamed to ask or being scared of the outcome, external obstacles that can range from the product/service not being up to standard. Replace the fear of being judged with personal belief and watch what happens. For example, when PR agencies reached out for us to interview guests on the show, Dan realized he might be able to make some money by charging them a fee. It seemed counterintuitive at the time because it'd make sense to pay the guest for their time, but for the value that he was providing, he thought it was worth exploring. To date, we've closed this type of sale more than twenty times and given people a voice through our platform. If he had just stayed with the mindset that he'll interview anyone who has a good background for free, the podcast wouldn't be sustainable and he'd never reap financial benefits if he didn't choose to apply courage, tenacity, and sticking to his guts.

Once you identify what stands in the way, devise a plan to solve these things or find someone who can help overcome them. It's not always enough to rely on sheer determination, it's important to be proactive and use unconventional methods to achieve results.

Overcoming Obstacles

There's something to be said about curiosity and its relationship with fear. Both come back to the mindset and while the former is associated with driving action, the latter is documented as the paralyzer of action. If there's one contrast at the helm of major business milestones, it's between the threshold of fear of failure and the curiosity that is accompanied by a growth mindset. Just because it's difficult, doesn't mean it's not worth doing.

Saying Yes to Fear

Meredith Whipple Callahan, a partner and executive coach for Evolution, writes in her book, *The Intentional Life*, to say yes to fear. When it comes to running a startup, not achieving desired outcomes is common and so are the fear of running out of money, not raising money, or not getting customers.

Our overall response to fear is saying no because we are against experiencing frustration, failure, etc. What if we told you the hack is shifting from a no to a yes so that fear stops taking up so much space in our lives? We give fear a lot of power because we spend time thinking, 'Yes! I might be alone for the rest of my life. Yes! I might not get this job. Yes! I am going to die someday.' Our orientation towards 'yes' actually dissipates that power of fear. The beauty is that as soon as you realize you can turn around and say 'Hi!', you expand your ability to be able to make all of the choices you want without having these dark corners of your life that you're trying to avoid.

Call it doubt, concern, apprehension, discomfort, or just fear itself. Accept the worst-case scenario and realize that admitting these things is not the end of the world, that you will be better off than where you started because the action has expelled the doubt and that an answer is more valuable than waiting around. The worst thing in the business world is nothing happening.

132   Startup Mindsets

Anxiety comes from living too far in the future or too far in the past. In an interview with Cari Jacobs-Crovetto, an executive coach, Dan learned that being completely present is the way to combat pressure and demands of running a business. In an uncertain work environment tied directly to your personal life, where you expect to rely on the income generated from the revenue or balance sheet to sustain your existence, one will be anxious. Dan found that what was often forcing him to doubt himself when he was selling podcast sponsorships over email was that this potential sale mattered so much because it would determine if the business was successful or not. He has learned that it is more efficient to not let anticipating a yes or a no affect his present perspective. Truly staying in the moment means not letting the future or past affect your current mindset. To do this, one must be incredibly present and focused on the moment.

Try this exercise:

1. Close your eyes
2. Inhale through your nose for five seconds
3. Hold for five seconds
4. Exhale slowly

Recalibrating your body and mind makes a tangible difference in how you're able to operate and do things that you could be overthinking.

Turn What Ifs to Even Ifs

When we mentally psych ourselves out about doing something that scares us, we tend to retreat from it. In our minds, we come up with a 'what if' scenario that makes us uncomfortable so we procrastinate and avoid the brunt of the decision. We may want to apply the courage needed but our bodies tense up into fight or flight mode, sometimes getting in the way of what we truly want.

Overcoming Obstacles 133

This is totally normal but it goes to show that the obstacle means something to you because it affects you, personally you might regret not making the move. It is important to harness these moments because they can be truly life-changing in the direction we desire.

By saying 'even if' instead of 'what if', we change the perspective of the sentence completely.

For example, say, 'Even if they give me the nastiest rejection, I will try again in another instance.' By conditioning our minds to be okay with an outcome instead of seeing it as the end of world, we can continually strive for the things that mean the most to us despite what fear we may experience.

In a vulnerable yet admirable LinkedIn post, Brain Potts uploaded a picture of his framed rejection letter from Perkins Cole twenty years ago when he was a second year student in 2022. Brian had become a partner at the very law firm that had denied him many years ago. When Dan asked him what had made the difference, he said it was just climbing the ladder. Brian eventually landed a role at Foley and Lardner.

As a second-year law student, Brian had applied to work at every one of the top hundred law firms in the country. He received rejection letters from all of them. Less than a decade later, Brian was among the youngest to make equity partner at one of those firms. And today, he's an equity partner at Perkins Cole—where his rejection letter from the firm in 2002 hangs on his office wall.

Since 2013, Brian has been ranked by Chambers USA and listed in The Best Lawyers in America and Wisconsin Super Lawyers. Best Lawyers also named him 'Lawyer of the Year' in the Energy Regulatory Law category in 2018 and 2020, and the firm named him co-chair of its hundred-plus lawyer Energy Industry Group in 2020.

Brian credits much of his success to his never-ending focus on writing and public speaking and returning to the mission of doing good for society.

134   Startup Mindsets

Brian's gone on to become a polymath with several businesses under his belt—notably Goods Unite Us, which has an ETF that trades on Nasdaq, the Legal Mentor Network, and a book called *The Jobless Lawyer's Handbook*.

The truth is, we never know which hit will cause a stone to crack, but science will show that the tide can turn. Obstacles are personal to us because we define what are obstacles whereas we can simply perceive them as opportunities. Yes, our egos hurt after hundreds of rejections and struggles but constant obsession over the tasks ahead may get you there. Each 'no' you receive builds humility, resilience, and leads the way to perseverance. There's a way to find joy in doing arduous tasks. Believe it or not, what appeals to our human mindset is the thrill of the chase.

Be Sand

In October 2023, Dan went to Brooklyn to meet up with a friend whom he had on the podcast, Ravi Kurani. Ravi's the founder of Sutro and an alumni of UC Riverside, but it was Dan's first time meeting him in person. Ravi shared stories of sleeping on friends' apartment couches while fundraising for Sutro in New York after being rejected by UC Riverside's investment committee. One thing that inspired Dan was Ravi mentioning he had spent USD 20,000 on his credit card for Sutro and the startup struggling to continue operating in its early days. Dan asked Ravi if he was scared that things would not work out at the time and he said, 'No. My family's still going to accept me back home. What are they going to do, not take me in if this fails?'

A few years later, Sutro would be acquired by Sani Marc, and Ravi credits his audacity and scrappiness to facing rejection after rejection. What goes untold and is often misunderstood from an outsider's perspective to entrepreneurship is the struggle but that same struggle creates the value of the success that is achieved.

Ravi taught Dan a visualization technique to get over some of the what ifs he had in his mind at the time.

Very carefully, he explained that when a rock gets a scratch on it and waves wash up on it, that scratch stays on the rock, however, when a line is drawn in the sand on the beach and the waves wash it up, the sand goes along with the waves and the line is not there any more. As humans, we hold on to past events like a badge of honour, but little do we know they are baggage holding us back from achieving our potential. Perhaps an experience in the past did not work out the way we wanted or we were harmed by what happened that influenced our mindsets towards thinking what we are currently attempting to do, creating a self-perceived wall in front of us. But what if we visualize a trampoline instead of a wall? How much easier would it be to commit to the action?

Does this guarantee results?

No, it does not but we need special optimism for the future so we can be energized to take action towards it. Do you feel with every fibre in your being that this is what you want to do? Are you determined in the face of adversity? Will you overcome the obstacles in your way?

15

It's a Marathon, Not a Sprint: Sustaining the Journey

'The game will test you but never fold. Stay ten toes down. It's not on you, it's in you, and what's in you, they can never take away.'

—Nipsey Hussle

Entrepreneurship is doing the task at hand, one by one, and not letting future expectations stop you from executing to the best of your ability. It's best to live in the moment, as there will be countless instances of pushing yourself past your limits. One hack that our friend René Morkos, whom we mentioned in Chapter 1, is to add five minutes more. By this we mean, when your mind wants to give up on a task, just add five minutes to your timer and don't leave the task until it ends. Doing this repeatedly for about five times builds resilience and commitment.

In a job market where hiring leans towards self-starters and those who've adapted to new technologies, it is important to apply a startup mindset when beginning anything new and out of your field of expertise. Anil Reddy, the founder of Lollipop Design, states that in this digital world with learning at our fingertips, it is incumbent on applicants to create their own design portfolio and learn by doing on their own instead of just applying for an internship without experience. The tech world rewards those who

138   Startup Mindsets

can be self-taught and find real-world applications. This means that people must go out of their way to learn and attain experience via an entrepreneurial avenue.

The Journey of a Thousand Miles Starts with a Single Step

What started out as a tiny device that would attach itself to the headphone jack of smartphones in early 2009, Jack Dorsey and Jim McCelvey began building out what we know today as Square. Square today is a company valued at USD 100 billion, doing 3 billion in annual revenue. They continued to innovate with the launch of new products. They were not just focused on hardware, and launched an extremely popular mobile payment application with Cash App.

Every little idea that eventually becomes a company starts out small. Ask yourself, what would happen if this became a ten-year ride and where would the company be in ten years? Yes, it's daunting to think about but ultimately, optimizing for a long runway and being in for the long haul means buckling up and steering the ship to milestone after milestone.

Jim developed a long model of serving economies of scale. For the many success stories we hear about, there are dozens more failures. While success is never guaranteed, great entrepreneurs and venture capitalists work together to reduce risk. It's an overnight success that takes ten years. Be sure that you're willing to stay the course, go through turbulence, and know the journey is always taking place.

The mindset dictates how you approach challenging or regular situations. While it will change throughout the course of your career/life, the ability to know how to think about overcoming obstacles and the mental fortitude demanded plays a big role in achieving great goals. It is our perception that dictates our reality.

In order to orient your mindset towards your goals, you must make sure that your actions will be able to meet your needs and serve customers at scale.

The act of getting paying customers is a turbulent journey full of highs and a shaky middle. We remember pitching paid sponsorships to startups to sponsor our podcast, *Startup Mindsets*, and wondering if anyone would say yes. Especially since our audience numbers did not seem as impressive with 7,000 total downloads total. But your numbers should not let you disregard the value you know your platform can bring. Always highlight the value that the numbers do not always show. Maybe it's the niche group of users who prioritize quality over quantity, one has to be able to appeal to each prospect uniquely.

For us at *Startup Mindsets*, it was that we were an emerging brand in the podcast space, highly reputable entrepreneurs would be on our podcast, and an audience of people interested in entrepreneurship. But if we could give any advice in this book, it is to keep going in the direction that challenges you personally because that is where the truth is found.

Like our friend, Will Peng, CEO of Northstar, says, 'Entrepreneurs seek out the truth.' They find out whether the market wants their product or service, whether investors will willingly fund their ideas. As an entrepreneur you must face the truth, embrace it, and yearn for it every step of your journey. Whether it's everyday tasks making decisions or facing the growth cramps that come with scaling, one must move forward. Remember there is always something you can do to enhance the current value of the product or service being offered. But, quoting Dickinson again, 'Tell the truth but tell it slant.' We must learn to perceive ourselves as worthy of the results we desire before we attain them. There is power in thinking that way because belief empowers us to act.

The Journey Is the Reward

Mindsets are built over time. You have to realize that you must evolve along with what the current throws your way. New challenges will come and test your limits. The most important thing is to believe and hope with utmost conviction, despite the consequences of falling short over and over again, that many things can go wrong while achieving a greater mission that enhances the lives of people.

Being an entrepreneur requires learning by doing and is not a spectator sport. There will be days that require many firsts, some things that you have never done before. While all that is mentioned above may sound daunting and resemble nothing of the traditional office structure work we are familiar with, just because it is difficult does not mean it is not worth doing. When a solution to a real-life problem resonates with you and thousands of others, there needs to be unconventional action that is oftentimes scary and uncomfortable to push things forward. The solution starts out with an idea, then hundreds if not thousands of actions that follow.

The Feeling of Pursuit

When the joy of being in the race captivates you, excites your inner being, then you know you are doing something you love and are almost bound to the goal you desire. It's somewhat comical that it can get lost in the mundane, day-to-day operational activities, as there are many hurdles on the route to success.

What's important to remember is that there will always be mountains to climb despite attaining that success. When you embrace the struggle and don't give a f#$k about it, you'll feel empowered to go after it.

The problem for many of us is that success ends with the first milestone whether it's considered raising funding or 1 million in revenue. We simply cannot stop because one goal is attained. Yes, there will be a day to retire and move on to new, important things but true growth is having the conviction for sticking to the journey for the long haul.

Daniel Stelmach and Nick Skrzyniarz, the founders of Changed, an app created for solving student loan crisis, found themselves on *Shark Tank* pitching Mark Cuban, Alex Rodriguez, and the sharks USD 250,000 for 15 per cent of their business. Nick admits to only doing USD 800 in revenue at the time and working as an Uber driver during the mornings and nights to have money to support himself and the company. On the podcast, we learned that Nick had a saying that goes, 'Embrace the broom.' It goes back to Ron Ro's point about trusting your story and embracing the honesty of the difficulty that accompanies operating and scaling a company.

The best reason to get into entrepreneurship is the solution you are providing is 100 per cent what you are passionate about and are uniquely able to provide an option that in your mind is better than what already exists. This will be anything but easy. Remember to champion rapidly testing out your product and welcoming good and bad user feedback.

At the end of the day, the real goal is to have a tangible impact on people's lives by solving their pain points or enhancing their capabilities. This is the mission of every new company that calls itself a startup seeking to contribute a verse in the world of technology and business. What matters most is being able to look back on your efforts one day and knowing something exists that drastically improved a challenge people faced.

You can take someone who's never done anything entrepreneurial before and help them discover that they enjoy doing their own thing. Applying entrepreneurial practices of valuing user feedback, iterating, optimizing for scale are things that serve the smallest to the largest endeavour. Remember to think global and start small.

Mindsets change and are not always constant, one day motivation will reach its peak while other times it will be very low. To say that anyone can sustain the mindset prescribed in this book over a long period of time would be inaccurate. As humans, we are constantly adapting and filtering what we want to believe and put into action. However, that doesn't mean this is all for nothing. The important lesson is to learn from our actions, thoughts, and decisions to be able to apply the best methodology for the obstacles both internally and externally in entrepreneurship.

One last thing, faith, courage, relentlessness, are not necessarily things that can be forced. They are intangibles found at the core of a person. It's not necessarily possible to teach someone to be courageous, since the act of courage occurs during the moment. The faith to take the leap and start a business with all hands on deck is an intrinsic characteristic. Yes, you can cultivate your mind any way you want but true passion is found within and we all have our own ways of discovering what it is. Remember to let your passion guide you while combining the mindset mentioned throughout this book.

Perhaps what we are chasing is this feeling inside of us when we know there is no doubt that we have given the task at hand everything we have. The joy of success in reaching our wildest dreams, that all the work we put in means something, proving to oneself that one is worthy of what one desires.

Epilogue
Final Thoughts

Why Earl Believes a Country like the Philippines Could Be a First World Country in Twenty-Five Years Through Embracing Their Own Startup Mindset

As Earl closes his final thoughts on this book, he has stepped into his new role as Executive Member of the National Innovation Council of the Philippines representing the entire business sector. He took his oath in front of the President and the public on 30 June 2023. Many asked him why he accepted the post, and all he could say was that he didn't want to wait until he retired to have a chance to help uplift the lives of 100 million people through what he knows best—building innovation ecosystems.

As many of you know, Earl has been blessed with an amazing career—growing up in Manila, having the chance to study in great academic institutions such as UP, Boston University, Cornell, and Stanford, and working in the heart of Silicon Valley and the New York tech ecosystems, and now having a chance to live his dream by being a co-founder of an AI and fintech startup with the Philippines as the pilot country. He wouldn't have imagined his life turning this way.

But as he turned forty-one, he realized that we all need to be thankful for our careers but also find a way to use them to create maximum impact for the world. Otherwise, what is the point of gaining all that experience if you don't share it? He could have waited until he was sixty-five or seventy to work in a council like this, but what came to his mind was always this: 'If not you, who? If not now, when?' and Jeff Bezos' challenge, 'The best choice you can make is to use your gifts and live a life of service and adventure. And your life will be defined by the choices you make as you author your life.'

Given these reflections, Earl is extremely optimistic that within the next twenty-five years, the Philippines can be a First World country again. That with leadership, guidance, alignment, and a bit of luck, it is possible.

Why is this? He has five reasons why he feels this way:

1. Getting global technical experience has been reset due to standardization of remote work. Given the changes in the past three to four years since the pandemic, access to global experience and projects has never been more accessible to Filipinos than ever before. Earl has seen dozens of startups hire remote teams and look at the Philippines to hire employees rather than outsource contract workers. With this, the technical experience and challenges that a technologist might solve could be the same as counterparts in Silicon Valley. Also, with the maturity of the tech ecosystem in Southeast Asia, there are many different digital-first employees who have years of experience, seeing how it is to grow from an idea to thousands of customers within a short time frame. This 'scale-up' experience typically only happened in places like Silicon Valley but has now been available to thousands of workers in a place like the Philippines.

2. There is no clear country leader in Generative AI, as everyone is starting at the same time. With the advent of OpenAI and tools like ChatGPT accessible to engineers

Epilogue 145

in the US and other parts of the world, the knowledge to work with this groundbreaking technology has no more 'time lag'. In the 2000s and 2010s, the latest tech innovation typically had a twelve-to-eighteen-month lag of being trained or dabbled in places not in the United States or Western Europe. These days, Earl sees that there is no time advantage to learn the latest Generative AI tech even if you are in Mumbai, Manila, or New York, thus it is hard to tell where the centre of gravity of talent, product, and know-how will be with this Generative AI phase especially driven on how regulation or the population is embracing this change. For example, his startup, Plentina,[20] is now experimenting with Generative AI and other machine learning models to help automate wealth management. This is being built by a collaboration between US and Filipino technical teams with the infrastructure of a hyperscaler like Google Cloud and tools like OpenAI.

3. The Philippines has the important metallic mineral resources that will power the batteries and chip industry. According to the Philippine Statistics Authority (PSA), critical minerals such as nickel, copper, and gold reserves are some of the highest in the world in the Philippines. With the shift in technology that needs more processing power and batteries, countries like the Philippines have the opportunity to move up the value chain and potentially add value to these minerals and take out potential middle men that just want to import the raw materials and post-process them in their countries. This move would be a huge shift for countries that have been historically just exploited for minerals but do not get most of the value.

4. The young and digital-first generation of the Philippines adopts trends faster than most of the world. With a median

---

[20] https://www.plentinafinancial.com/.

age 24.5, and a 100 million population, the country will have most of its workforce born in or experiencing the internet through their mobile phones their entire lives. Because of this, adoption and potential creation of new technologies can be piloted in the Philippines but can quickly scale to markets where there is also mostly the same generational cohort. With digital adoption crossing borders faster than ever, it would not come as a surprise that a product that is built in a place like the Philippines can be adopted somewhere else.

5. If we can focus as a country to be global leaders in three to five areas, the nation can succeed. In the 1960s, during the Cold War, the United States grew a national battle cry to bring America to the moon first with NASA and the Apollo missions. Everyone wanted to contribute to this big mission. Countries like the Philippines need the same focus as a nation, to fix a big generational goal that the whole country can solve and lead the world. Some areas that make sense for the Philippines, for example, are climate change tech to help solve the disasters that the country is faced with every year, and then advise other markets how to do this; addressing food security or growing technology that will supercharge the agriculture and aquaculture capability of the country, then export these technologies to other markets. One last area is in data-driven financial services, where we can create new models to help the population grow their financial capability as the income economy to an upper middle economy by 2025, which means more services not merely in spending or credit but also focusing on payments, savings wealth building, or investing.

For the next three years of Earl's appointment to be part of the National Innovation Council, he is looking forward to working

Epilogue 147

with the President, the Cabinet Members, and the seven Executive Members from the private sector to have a chance to serve the Filipino people. He will do his part to help move the country forward by building programmes and policies that will strengthen the innovation capability of the country and unlock our shared mission that maybe in our lifetimes, we can see an emerging market like the Philippines regain its prominence as a First World country and a top twenty global economy by mid-century.

Conclusion

What will your next step be? What action will you take after reading this book? Have you crystallized and written your own personal mission and goals? The world is waiting for you to start and create the impact that you are destined for.

Life is short, regret looms longer. Take the leap, and we are excited to see what amazing things you'll be creating using your very own startup mindsets.

Acknowledgements

The authors would like to thank the Penguin Random House Southeast Asian team, led by Nora Nazarene Abu Bakar, for believing in our book as one of the major advocates for the authors in the region to tell our stories and experiences to the world. For our editors such as Cassandra Chia, thank you for patiently giving us first-time authors feedback to make our book better. We greatly appreciate you giving authors like us a voice in a world where it's about time that our region amplifies our own.

To all the podcast guests we have interviewed over the course of four years, thank you for sharing your stories, entertaining our questions, and being dear friends. You all have truly played an instrumental role in the creation of this book and sources of inspiration for us and readers, knowing the adversities you've overcome.

Lastly, the authors would like to thank all the mentors, teachers, and advocates who have helped them throughout their careers, in giving them guidance and inspiration throughout their journey. They will be forever grateful for sharing their wisdom and helping shape their lives because of their time and their advice.

From Earl

I would like to acknowledge the tremendous support of my family, especially my wife, Patty, who has been my cheerleader and inspiration from day one. She has always challenged me to chase after my dreams and always been my thought partner in all the crazy risky life decisions that I have made throughout my life. Since we met in grade school, you have always been the benchmark of what my perfect girl is and I am glad that the universe made a chance that summer to let us reconnect again. You are the one who pushed me to write this book and continue to keep on pushing forward in life.

For my children, Rocco, Maxwell, and Alexis, I am amazed everyday how you are growing in every part of your life. I know that having a dad as an entrepreneur is not as easy compared to some of your classmates, who have stable lives, but I always thank you for the understanding and patience as your dad pursues his life goals. Every keystroke I typed in this book, I hope, will inspire more people to pursue positive change in the world and bring a better future for your generation.

I would like to thank my parents, Edgardo and Agnes, and my siblings, Kuys E and Ails. Since I was a child, you have pushed me towards my journey, from thinking that I will end up being a dinosaur explorer, astronaut, or an entrepreneur, you have not limited what I could try to become in life. The lessons that you have given me serve as the guiding principles of my life decisions. Also, I would like to thank my in-laws, Benjie, Lyn, and F.R.O. Oliva, who have been instrumental in keeping the family set despite the volatility of entrepreneurship.

Even if they have both passed away, I would like to show my greatest appreciation to my grandfather whom I never met, Lolo Brigido Valencia, and my grandmother, Lola Bi-ing Valencia, who taught me that dreaming of being both a successful businessman and a public servant in one's lifetime is possible if you have a singular focus. I thank you for passing on the values of hard work, patience, and the value of giving back and fighting for change in a country like the Philippines on which many citizens have given up on already.

Acknowledgements 151

From Dan

To my father, Roland, whom I lost in 2021, I wouldn't be here without you letting me dream and being a pillar of unwavering support. I am forever grateful. To my mother, Elizabeth, thank you for everything, this book is truly as much a credit to you than my individual effort.

To my cousin, attorney, Jim Narvios, you've inspired me to believe in myself and take chances that could propel my life forward especially when I felt stuck, lost, and hopeless. To my good friend Jovanni, this wouldn't be possible without your continued support over the years, like letting me borrow your laptop to write this, your friendship has been invaluable. To my homie, Brandon, we've come a long way since Google, thank you for helping me get here.